BIBLE HISTORY ATLAS

F. F. Bruce

BIBLE HISTORY ATLAS

Popular Study Edition

CROSSROAD · NEW YORK

Design and Art Work: Rivka Myers
Cartography: Lorraine Kessel
Copyright © 1982, F.F. Bruce and Carta, Jerusalem

The Crossroad Publishing Company
575 Lexington Avenue
New York, NY 10022

Library of Congress Catalog Card No. 81-71183√

ISBN 0-8245-0418-6

Printed in Israel

TABLE OF CONTENTS

MAPS

IN THE BEGINNING

(Genesis 1–11)

The Bible opens with an account of how God created the universe, and goes on to give a description of the infancy of the human race. It tells how the first human pair lived in the garden of Eden, a kind of oasis in a vast desert area. Eden is said to lie in the east – that is, probably, east from the Holy Land. Its position is shown more precisely by reference to four rivers in its neighbourhood. We cannot say for sure which two rivers were the Pishon and the Gihon, but the two others bear well-known names, the Tigris and the Euphrates. These are the two great rivers of the land which we know today as Iraq. Somewhere in that direction, then, Eden was situated.

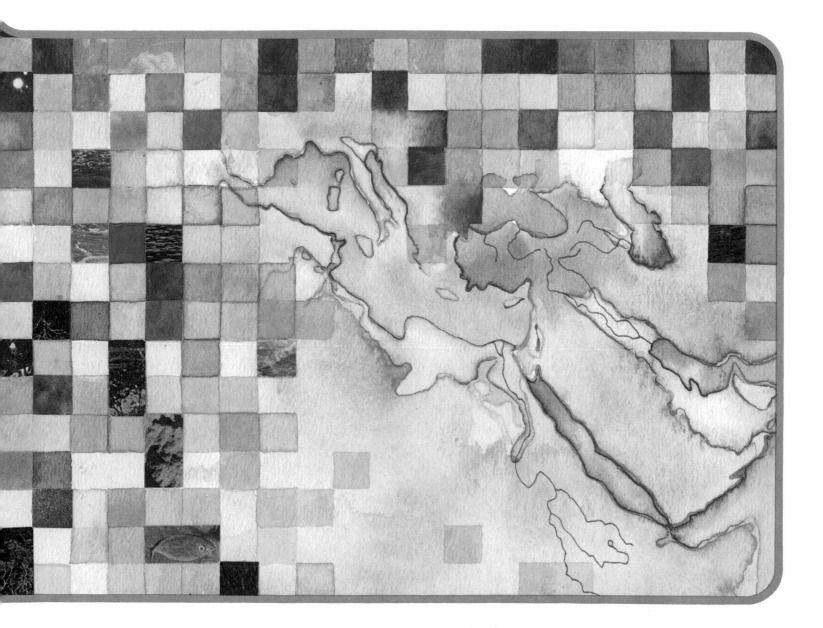

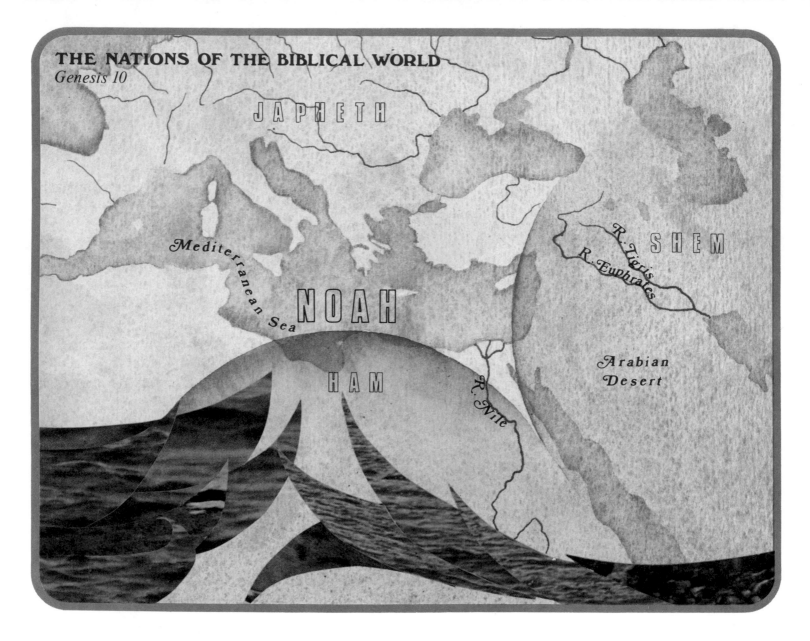

JAPHETH

Mediterranean Sea

SHEM

R. Tigris

R. Euphrates

NOAH

HAM

Arabian Desert

R. Nile

From living as food-gatherers in Eden its residents moved out to become food-producers – herdsmen and farmers. The clash between the pastoral and the farming ways of life is illustrated in the story of Abel, the shepherd, and Cain, the farmer. As time went on, yet another way of life made its appearance – city life. Cain is said to have built a city and called it Enoch, after the name of his son.

There were many strong cities in the Near East from about 7000 BC onwards. People started to build cities such as Jericho even before they learned the art of pottery. This was during the Neolithic or New Stone Age. Between it and the Bronze Age, which began shortly before 3000 BC there was a phase known as the Chalcolithic Age.

From about 4300 BC onwards, there were several fine cities in the Euphrates Valley. The civilization that was swept away in the great flood of Noah's day was based on city life – what we call an urban civilization.

The only geographical detail in the story of Noah's flood comes at the end, where the ark in which he and his family escaped from drowning is said to have settled among the mountains of Ararat – that is, Armenia. But that is sufficient to "place" the flood in the valley of the Euphrates and Tigris: these rivers have their source in Armenia. There is literary and archaeological evidence of a number of great floods in the Euphrates-Tigris valley, but we cannot be sure that any of those was the flood described in the book of Genesis. The Genesis flood was like those others, but apparently more devastating in its effects.

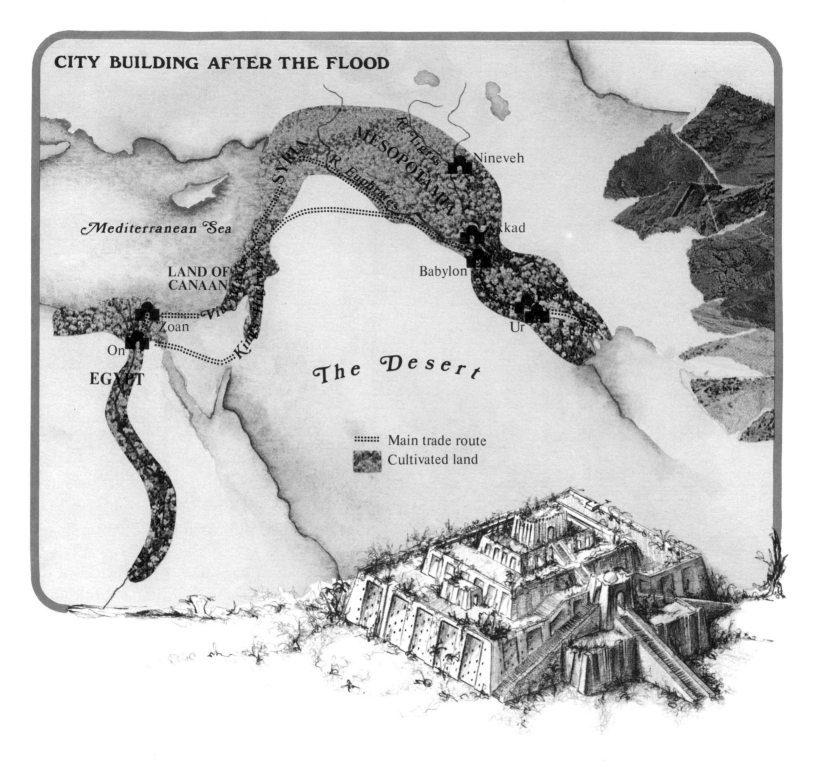

CITY BUILDING AFTER THE FLOOD

After the waters had subsided and people were able to return to the flooded area, there was a fresh wave of city-building. Several of the cities built or rebuilt at this time are mentioned in Genesis 10: Babylon, Erech (Uruk) and Akkad in the Euphrates basin and Nineveh and others on the Tigris. The Bible links some of these with Nimrod, ''a mighty hunter before the Lord''.

The story of the tower of Babel in Genesis 11 has to do with the great ziggurat or stepped temple-tower of Babylon, which was ascended by a sloping ramp. These ziggurats are thought to have been built to imitate the mountains on which immigrants into the Euphrates valley had worshipped their gods in the highland country from which they came. The Babylonians called this tower Etemenanki, which means ''house of the foundation-platform of heaven and earth''. If this means that it was seen as a symbolical link between heaven and earth, it reminds us of the builders' words: ''Come, let us build ourselves a city, and a tower with its top in the heavens''.

THE PATRIARCHS
AND THEIR WANDERINGS
(Genesis 12 – Exodus 1)
2000–1500 BC

Another important ziggurat was that of Ur, a city on the Euphrates about 150 miles south-east of Babylon, originally founded by people from the east called Sumerians. The first signs of human settlement on the site of Ur are dated about 4300 BC. The city was most prosperous under the Third Dynasty of Ur, established by King Ur-nammu shortly before 2000 BC. It was he who built the ziggurat; it stood within a large area consecrated to the worship of the moon-god.

Under the Third Dynasty Ur became the leading city in Southern Babylonia and the greatest commercial capital that the world had thus far seen. The dynasty lasted for just over 100 years; it collapsed under attacks from westerners known as Amorites. It was probably in the later phase of this dynasty that Abraham lived in Ur; his departure from the city may have taken place in the troubled years at the end of the dynasty. We do not know if Abraham was previously a worshipper of the moon-god, like most of his fellow-citizens; we do know that, after he was granted a revelation of the living and true God, he worshipped him alone.

From Ur Abraham and his family migrated north as far as Haran in the upper Euphrates valley. The name Haran means something like ''main road'' or ''cross-roads''; it lay on the crossroads of caravan routes running north and south with others running east and west. It carried on a regular trade with Ur, and through Ur with more distant parts; through Haran passed also caravans of traders between Assyria and Cappadocia (in Asia Minor) and between Elam (Persia) and Egypt (via Syria). Like Ur, Haran was specially devoted to the worship of the moon-god.

Abraham and his family stayed in Haran until Terah, his father, died; then the call of God directed him to set out on his further journeyings. Accompanied, therefore, not only by his wife Sarah but also by his nephew Lot with their flocks, herds and servants, Abraham travelled south-west through Syria until he came into the land then called Canaan.

Abraham and those who went with him were herdsmen, moving from centre to centre on the north-south road which led through Canaan. Shechem in central Canaan, where he built his first altar after arriving in the country, Mamre (near Hebron) in what was later the territory of Judah, and Beersheba in the Negeb are mentioned as places where he settled for longer or shorter periods.

On one occasion he went down into Egypt to escape from a famine in Canaan, and returned richer in flocks and herds than when he had gone down. The king of Egypt at the time was probably one of the rulers of the Twelfth Dynasty, whose capital was near Memphis, about 12 miles south of Cairo, on the west bank of the Nile. On another occasion Abraham spent some time in Gerar, a Canaanite city near the Egyptian border, the head-quarters of a king named Abimelech. In both Egypt and Gerar Abraham ran into difficulties by introducing Sarah as his sister. She was a blood-relation of his on his father's side, and in Haran she was legally his sister before she became his wife.

Mamre appears to have been Abraham's main residence in Canaan. Probably it was there that he left his household on occasions when he visited other centres in the course of his pastoral business. The oak or terebinth of Mamre, under which he once ''entertained angels unawares'', was still shown to visitors in the early centuries of the Christian era.

Mamre is about $1\frac{2}{3}$ miles from Hebron. The modern city of Hebron has grown up around the sacred enclosure built by King Herod around the traditional tombs of Abraham and his family. Abraham bought the field containing the cave of Machpelah (the ''double cave'') to serve as a burying-place for his wife Sarah; there he himself was later buried by his sons Ishmael and Isaac. In the next generation Isaac and his wife Rebecca were buried there, and a generation later Jacob and his elder wife Leah were buried there in their turn. (The site of Rachel's tomb is pointed out today at the side of the road leading from Bethlehem to Jerusalem.)

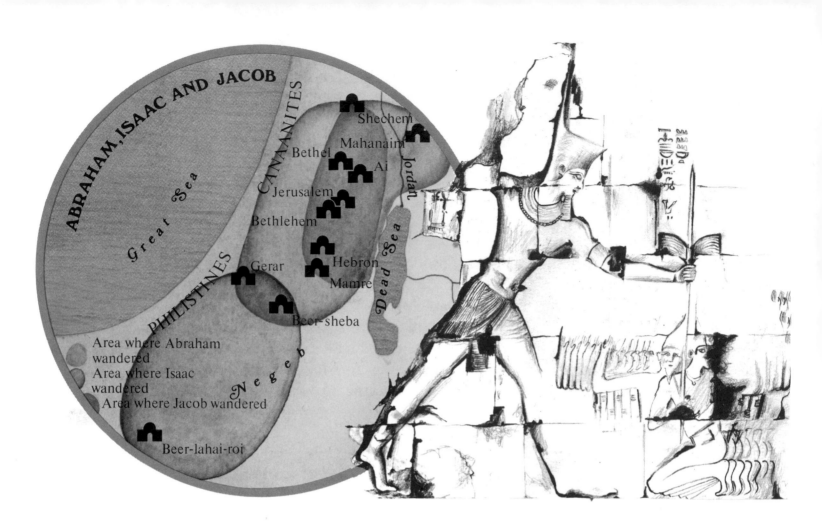

Isaac, Abraham's son, is specially associated with Beer-sheba, although he settled for periods in other places, including Gerar. Rebecca, his wife, came from the neighbourhood of Haran, from the city of Nahor. When the time came for Isaac to marry, Abraham sent a trusted servant to choose a wife for him among those relatives, rather than let him marry a Canaanite woman. In the next generation Esau, elder son of Isaac and Rebecca, married two Canaanite women, "daughters of Heth", who proved a sore trial to Rebecca. His brother Jacob, however, journeyed to Haran, where he married his mother's two nieces, Leah and Rachel. Most of Jacob's sons, the ancestors of the twelve tribes of Israel, seem to have taken Canaanite wives. His son Joseph married the daughter of an Egyptian priest.

Jacob spent twenty years in northern Mesopotamia, keeping sheep for his uncle and father-in-law Laban. On his return to Canaan he followed the same pastoral way of life as his father and grandfather. He was living near Hebron on the occasion when he sent his favourite son Joseph to Shechem to visit his other sons, who were keeping his sheep. When Joseph arrived at Shechem, he found that his brothers had departed for Dothan, some 20 miles farther north. It was there that they sold Joseph to travelling merchants who took him down to Egypt and sold him to an officer of the king of Egypt.

At this time Egypt was ruled by a dynasty of Asian invaders, known as the Hyksos. Their capital was at Avaris, in the eastern Delta. There Joseph, after several years, reached a position of great influence at the royal court. When his father and brothers and their families were forced by famine to leave Canaan for Egypt, as Abraham had once done, he arranged for them to settle in the eastern Delta, near the Asian frontier, in the district which the Bible calls Goshen.

It was natural to go to Egypt when Canaan and neighbouring countries were hit by famine. Egypt's fertility depends, not on an uncertain rainfall, but on the Nile, which rose annually and flooded the land on either side, so that it yielded abundant crops. Even the

Nile occasionally failed to rise and flood the land adequately, as during the seven years of famine in Joseph's time, but such periods of disaster were rare.

Ancient Egypt was made up of two main areas, which were originally separate kingdoms – the northern kingdom (Lower Egypt), consisting mainly of the Delta, and the southern kingdom (Upper Egypt), consisting of the strip of fertile territory on either side of the Nile between Cairo and Aswan. With the union of these two kingdoms about 3000 BC the succession of historical Egyptian dynasties begins. Some of those dynasties ruled from Memphis or its vicinity; others ruled from Thebes in Upper Egypt (the modern Luxor).

There were regular migrations from Asia into Egypt, usually peaceful. A painting in the rock-tomb of a governor at Beni-Hassan in Middle Egypt shows a party of nomads from Asia who arrived in Egypt shortly after 1900 BC. Their leader is called a "desert chieftain"; he is accompanied by women and children. They appear to have been wandering tinkers and musicians, and traded in black eye-paint which they brought from Transjordan.

Less peaceful was the invasion of the Hyksos about 1720 BC. They established themselves as rulers of Egypt for 150 years. The kings of the Eighteenth Dynasty expelled them and pursued them back into Canaan and Syria, winning a powerful empire there.

The kings of the Eighteenth Dynasty ruled from Thebes. But one king, Akhnaton (1379–1362 BC), abandoned Thebes and built a new capital at Akhetaton, east of the Nile (modern Tell el-Amarna). Here he encouraged the monotheistic worship of Aton, the kindly god of the sun's disk. When he was succeeded by his son-in-law Tutankhamun, the court returned to Thebes and the religious reformation of the "heretic king", as Akhnaton is sometimes called, was undone.

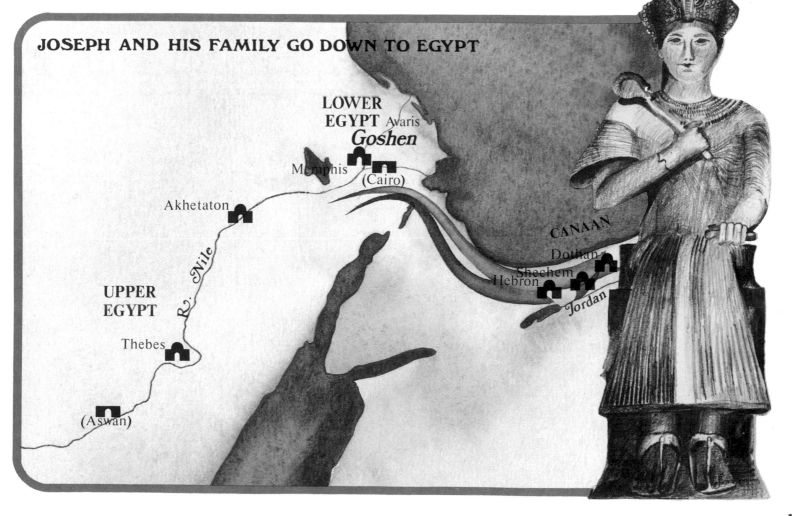

JOSEPH AND HIS FAMILY GO DOWN TO EGYPT

LOWER EGYPT Avaris
Goshen
Memphis
(Cairo)
Akhetaton
UPPER EGYPT
R. Nile
CANAAN
Dothan
Shechem
Hebron
Jordan
Thebes
(Aswan)

MOSES AND THE EXODUS FROM EGYPT

(Exodus 1–40)

1300–1200 BC

When the royal court moved back from Akhetaton to Thebes, after Akhnaton's death, the site of Akhnaton's capital was abandoned. Archaeologists were helped to identify the site by the accidental discovery in 1887 of the contents of Akhnaton's record office – clay documents popularly known as the Tell el-Amarna tablets.

These records preserve the correspondence between Pharaoh's court and his governors and vassal-kings in Canaan. They give a clear picture of the weakening of Egyptian power in Canaan and Syria. The rulers of the Hittite Empire, north of Syria, were persuading some of Egypt's vassals to change their allegiance. Elsewhere the rulers of some Canaanite city-states were declaring their independence, while in other parts havoc was being caused by raiders called the Habiru. This term seems to be indentical with the biblical term "Hebrews" – a broader term than "Israelites". If all Israelites were Hebrews (Habiru), not all Hebrews were Israelites. The Israelites' neighbours commonly referred to them as Hebrews, but in so doing they were referring to them as members of a wider grouping than Israelites.

The Habiru of the Tell el-Amarna tablets are not the Israelites who were in Egypt, but the Egyptian authorities may have come to suspect that the Israelites living within their frontiers were hand-in-glove with the troublesome Habiru in Asia. They might be waiting to stir up disorder in Egypt. The authorities therefore took steps to repress them.

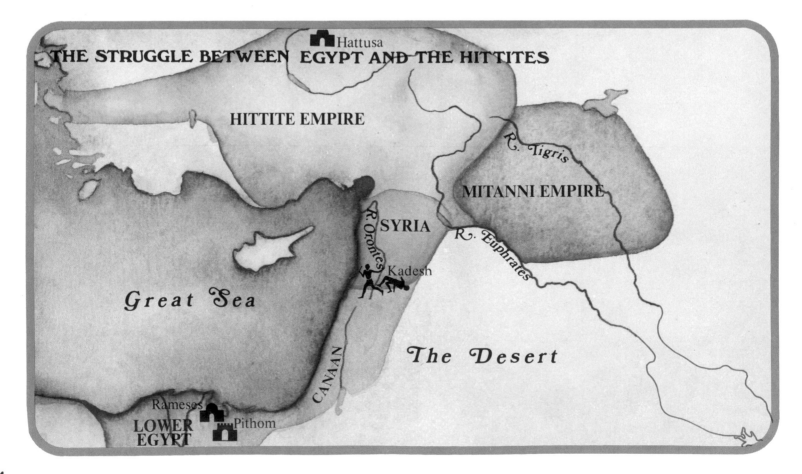

The repression became specially severe with the establishment of the Nineteenth Dynasty, which maintained its court in Lower Egypt. The chief king of this dynasty was Rameses II (1300–1234 BC). His efforts to regain the empire which his predecessors had lost in Asia brought him into conflict with the Hittites, with whom he fought a memorable battle at Kadesh on the Orontes in the fifth year of his reign. Rameses claims an overwhelming victory, but the battle was indecisive. Some time later Rameses received a daughter of the Hittite king in marriage.

Rameses is widely believed to have been the Pharaoh who drafted the Israelites into forced labour gangs to build his new cities. One of the cities which they are said to have built for Pharaoh bears the name Rameses (Raamses). This is probably the city known to the Egyptians as Pi-Ramesse (''the house of Rameses''), the site of which has been identified quite recently in the eastern Delta, not far from the former Hyksos capital of Avaris.

The Israelites naturally found this way of life an unwelcome change from their pastoral existence. They endured their oppression for at least a generation before they found a deliverer in the person of Moses.

Moses was by birth one of themselves, although he bore an Egyptian name and, by a strange combination of circumstances, had been brought up at the Egyptian court. Under his leadership the Israelites were able at last to leave Egypt for the wilderness of Sinai.

Moses himself had spent some years in that wilderness. The king found reason to suspect that Moses was minded to champion the oppressed Israelites, and Moses had to leave Egypt in a hurry. During his exile in the wilderness of Sinai, Moses had the strange experience at the ''burning bush'' in which the God of his ancestors, Abraham, Isaac and Jacob, spoke to him. He introduced himself to Moses by the name Yahweh, and commanded him to return to Egypt and lead his fellow-Israelites out to worship him there at the foot of the mountain variously called Sinai or Horeb.

By this time Rameses II was dead; his son and successor Merneptah was a weaker character. Moses faced him with Yahweh's demand to him to let his people go and worship

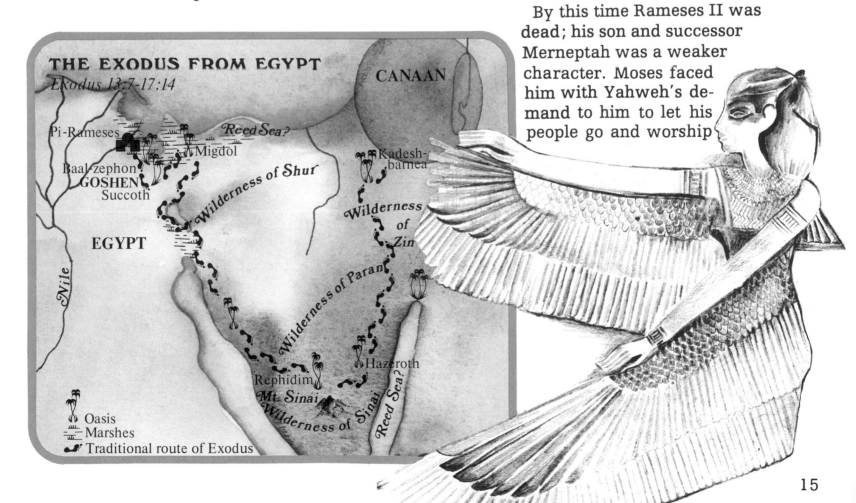

THE EXODUS FROM EGYPT
Exodus 13:7–17:14

CANAAN

Pi-Rameses
Reed Sea?
Migdol
Baal-zephon
GOSHEN
Succoth
Kadesh-barnea
Wilderness of Shur

EGYPT

Wilderness of Zin

Nile

Wilderness of Paran

Hazeroth
Rephidim
Mt. Sinai
Wilderness of Sinai
Reed Sea?

Oasis
Marshes
Traditional route of Exodus

15

him in the wilderness. At first the new king refused to acknowledge the authority of Yahweh, a god of whom he had never heard before; but as time went on he was compelled to recognize Yahweh's power. In the end he admitted that the successive disasters which befell his people and his land were signs of Yahweh's displeasure and showed himself only too glad to get rid of the Israelites.

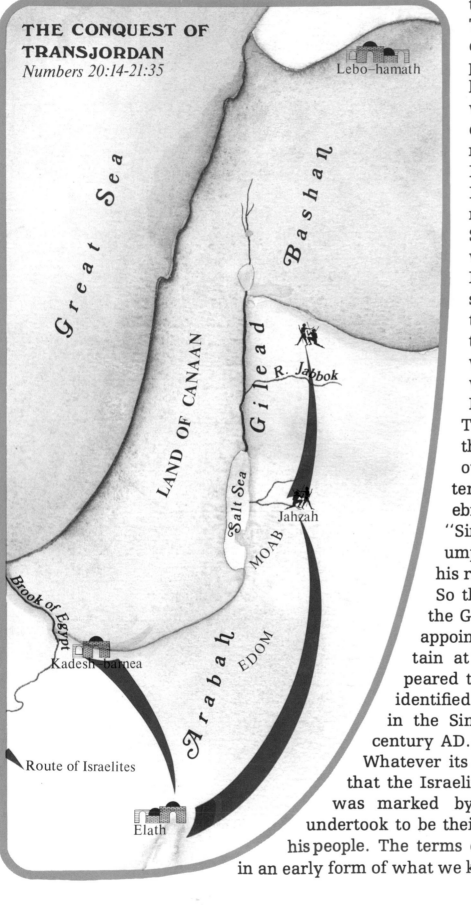

THE CONQUEST OF TRANSJORDAN
Numbers 20:14-21:35

Lebo–hamath

Great Sea

Bashan

LAND OF CANAAN

Gilead

R. Jabbok

Salt Sea

Jahzah

MOAB

Brook of Egypt

Kadesh–barnea

Arabah

EDOM

Route of Israelites

Elath

They, however, recognized these disasters as signs of Yahweh's powerful intervention on their behalf. The final sign of Yahweh's championship was the east wind which, just at the right moment, caused the "Sea of Reeds" to go back. The "Sea of Reeds" appears to have been a northern extension of the Red Sea. It blocked their way as they were leaving Egypt, and an Egyptian chariot force was pursuing them from behind, because the king had repented of letting them go. There seemed to be no way out of this trap when the water went back and, led by Moses, they advanced forward. The chariots, trying to follow them, were bogged down and overwhelmed by the returning water. This great deliverance was celebrated in the Song of the Sea: "Sing to Yahweh, for he has triumphed gloriously; the horse and his rider he has thrown into the sea." So they went on to the place where the God of their fathers had made an appointment with them, to the mountain at the foot of which he had appeared to Moses. No one seems to have identified Sinai or Horeb with Jebel Musa in the Sinai Peninsula before the fourth century AD.

Whatever its position, it was at Mount Sinai that the Israelites became a nation. This event was marked by a covenant, in which Yahweh undertook to be their God and they undertook to be his people. The terms of the covenant were expressed in an early form of what we know as the Ten Commandments.

These are commandments given by the God of Israel to his people, and he identifies himself in the introduction to the commandments: "I am Yahweh your God, who brought you out of the land of Egypt, out of the house of bondage." It is because he had done this for them that he required their devotion to be given to him alone, as the first commandment goes on to say: "You shall have no other gods before me" (that is, "in my presence").

In a religious ceremony held at the foot of the mountain the people accepted the covenant to be the law of their national and personal life. The law dealt with relations between persons and families within the nation; it also laid down the nation's religious and moral duties. Besides the divine commandments given in the "You shall..." style there later grew up a system of case-laws beginning with such a phrase as "If a man...". These case-laws, which were similar to some in the law-codes of other ancient Near Eastern nations, laid down guide-lines for life in a simple agricultural society. Such was the Israelites' society when first they settled down after their period of wandering in the wilderness. As society developed, both the social and the religious laws were developed further. For example, the tent or tabernacle, which served as their sanctuary in the wilderness and for some time after their settlement in Canaan, was later replaced by a more permanent structure (see pages 26, 27, 34). The rules about the sanctuary and its services had therefore to be altered as the situation changed.

On Mount Nebo, in Transjordan, after looking out across what was to become the land of Israel, Moses died, having won a secure place for himself among the pioneers of world civilization. The law-code which bears his name has been described as a monument more lasting than the Pyramids.

WHAT MOSES SAW
FROM MOUNT NEBO
Deuteronomy 34

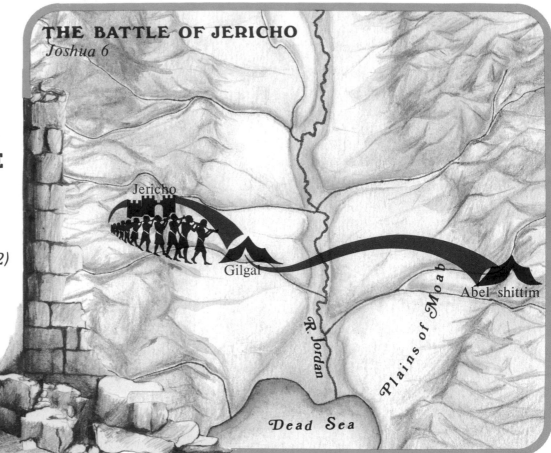

THE BATTLE OF JERICHO
Joshua 6

Jericho

Gilgal

Abel-shittim

R. Jordan

Plains of Moab

Dead Sea

JOSHUA AND THE CONQUEST OF CANAAN

(Joshua 1–24; Judges 1–2)
c. 1200 BC

A generation passed between the Israelites' departure from Egypt and their settlement in Canaan. The greater part of this interval was spent in the oasis of Kadesh-barnea, near the southern border of Canaan (see map, p. 15). From here some began to move into the Negeb, while the main body travelled east and north into Transjordan and crossed into Canaan from there.

Moses was succeeded as leader of the Israelites by Joshua, who stands out in the Bible story not as a law-giver but as a conqueror.

Jericho, 4½ miles west of the Jordan and 10 miles north of the Dead Sea, was the first place in Canaan to be taken by the Israelites under Joshua. It had been a walled city 6000 years before Joshua's time.

The city which stood there in Joshua's day was Late Bronze Age Jericho. It was smaller than some of the more elaborate cities which had stood there earlier. When it was destroyed by the Israelites, the site lay abandoned for three or four centuries, and wind, rain and sun have almost totally destroyed the remains of Joshua's Jericho.

From Jericho the invaders pressed on into the centre of the country, taking one citadel after another, for the news of the fall of Jericho had struck fear into the hearts of many Canaanite garrisons.

The next citadel to fall to the Israelites after Jericho, according to the Bible record, was Ai. Ai is identified with the great mound of Et-Tell, about 1½ miles east by south-east of Beitin (the ancient Bethel). Since Ai means simply "ruin", it is not surprising that the Israelites who saw the great mound called it "The ruin". The last settlement on Et-Tell was destroyed 1000 years before Joshua: it is not yet clear how this evidence fits in with the written evidence in the Bible.

The city of Gibeon, in the central hill-country, 7 or 8 miles north of Jerusalem, decided to play for safety and made peace with the invaders. This was regarded as an act of treachery by the neighbouring cities, and five of these, led by the king of Jerusalem, joined forces to attack Gibeon, but suffered a decisive defeat at Joshua's hands in the Pass of Beth-horon, a few miles north-west of Gibeon. This was the occasion when the sun is said to have "stood still" to enable Joshua to complete his victory.

The Israelites were unable to wage war successfully in the plains and valleys, where the chariotry of the Canaanite city-states was too strong for them to face. Before long, however, they conquered and occupied the hill-country of the centre and south, and also the Galilean uplands, north of the Plain of Jezreel. The decisive stroke in the conquest of the north was the storming of the great city of Hazor, "formerly", says the book of Joshua, "the head of all those kingdoms". Hazor is one of several fortified places shown by archaeological research to have fallen around 1200 BC and to have been rebuilt a few decades later with thinner walls and a less prosperous way of life.

In other places local groups took military action. In the central region Bethel was taken by members of the "house of Joseph". Shechem, over 20 miles north of Bethel, does not appear to have been captured at all, perhaps because it was already occupied by a population friendly or related to the Israelites.

Into the southern part of the country the tribes of Judah and Simeon moved in from the south, together with some allied groups such as the Kenizzites. The most outstanding Kenizzite was Caleb, who staked a claim to Hebron on an earlier visit when he went up from Kadesh-barnea with others to "spy out" the land. Now he made good his claim by capturing Hebron and the surrounding territory from those who then occupied it. Another famous Kenizzite was Othniel, Caleb's son-in-law, who later repelled an invasion of that part of Canaan mounted by a chief called Cushan-risha-thaim. The Kenizzites were in due course adopted into the tribe of Judah.

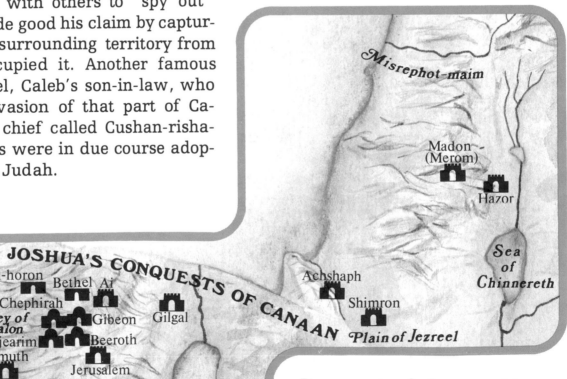

JOSHUA'S CONQUESTS OF CANAAN

Misrephot-maim
Madon (Merom)
Hazor
Sea of Chinnereth
Achshaph
Shimron
Plain of Jezreel

Beth-horon
Bethel Ai
Chephirah
Valley of Ayalon
Gibeon
Gilgal
Kiriath-jearim
Beeroth
Jarmuth
Jerusalem
Azekah
Libnah
Lachish
Eglon
Hebron
Gaza
Debir
Negeb
Dead Sea
Shephelah

Gibeonite city in league with Joshua
Canaanite city defeated by Joshua

It was not only by armed invasion and conquest that the Israelites established their position in Canaan. More often they were content to live alongside the local inhabitants, to marry into their communities and to adopt their religious customs. The fact that this tendency was so severely condemned by the prophets shows how wide-spread it was.

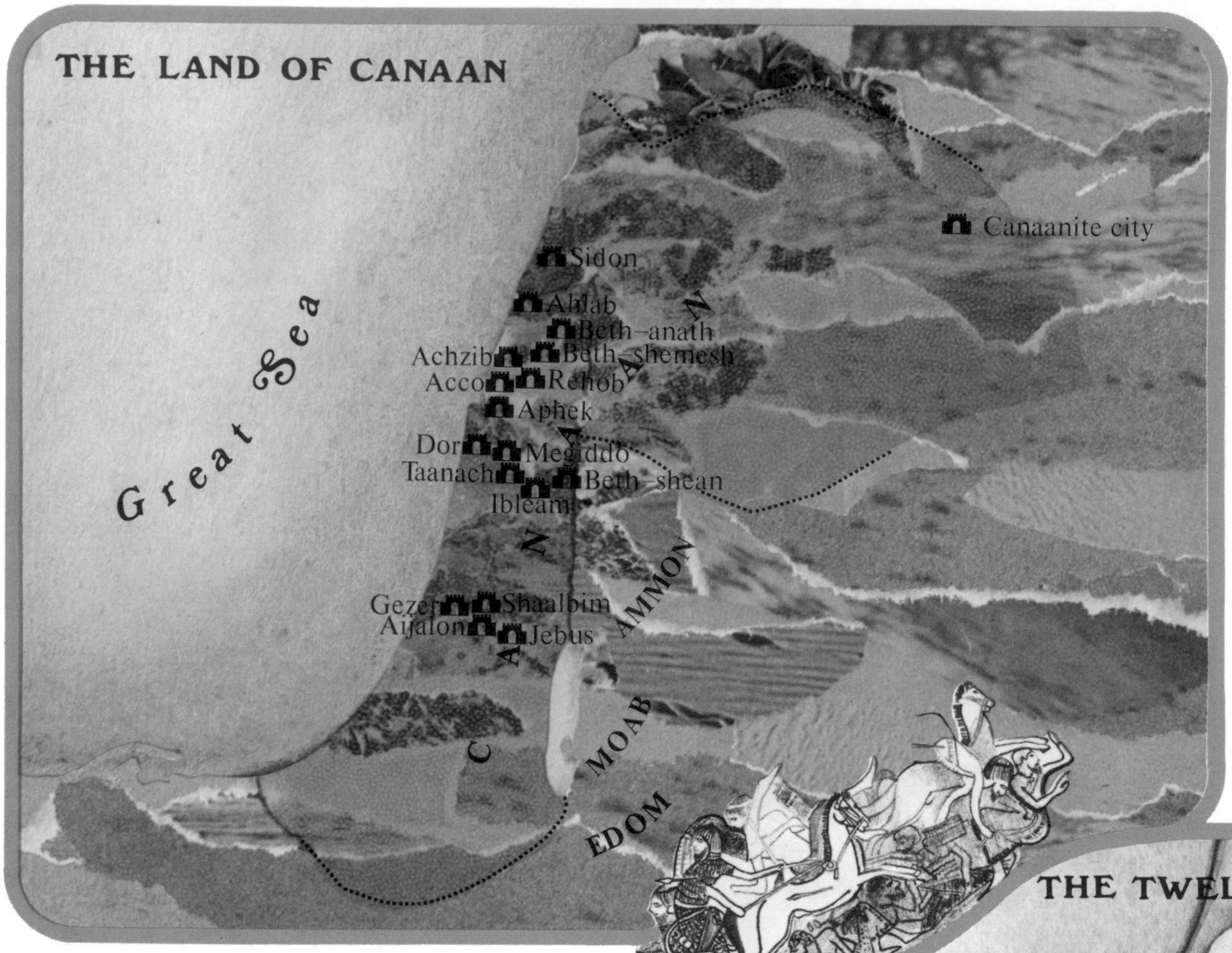

THE LAND OF CANAAN

Canaanite city

Sidon
Ahlab
Beth-anath
Achzib
Beth-shemesh
Acco
Rehob
Aphek
Dor
Megiddo
Taanach
Beth-shean
Ibleam
Gezer
Shaalbim
Aijalon
Jebus

Great Sea

C A N A A N

AMMON

MOAB

EDOM

THE TWELVE TRIBES

Great Sea

ASHER
NAPHTALI
DAN
ZEBULUN
ISSACHAR
MANASSEH
DAN
EPHRAIM
GAD
BENJAMIN
JUDAH
REUBEN
Dead Sea
SIMEON

Full shading: area under Israelite control
Partial shading: area outside Israelite control

The Canaanites were able for long to maintain their power in the lowlands, especially in the Plain of Jezreel, where a chain of fortified cities, strung out from west to east, largely cut off the northern tribes of Israel from those in the centre of the country. Between the central tribes and the territory of Judah farther south, the city of Jebus (later Jerusalem) remained as a Canaanite stronghold until the reign of David.

The division of the nation into twelve tribes belongs to the earliest period of national life. The twelve tribes claimed descent from the twelve sons of Jacob, but the names of the tribes are not always the same as those of Jacob's sons. The twelve tribes as usually reckoned included, as separate groups, Manasseh and Ephraim, two sections of the ''house of Joseph''. These two powerful tribes dominated the central highlands: Manasseh, indeed, extended east into Transjordan, occupying territory that had formerly belonged to Og, king of Bashan.

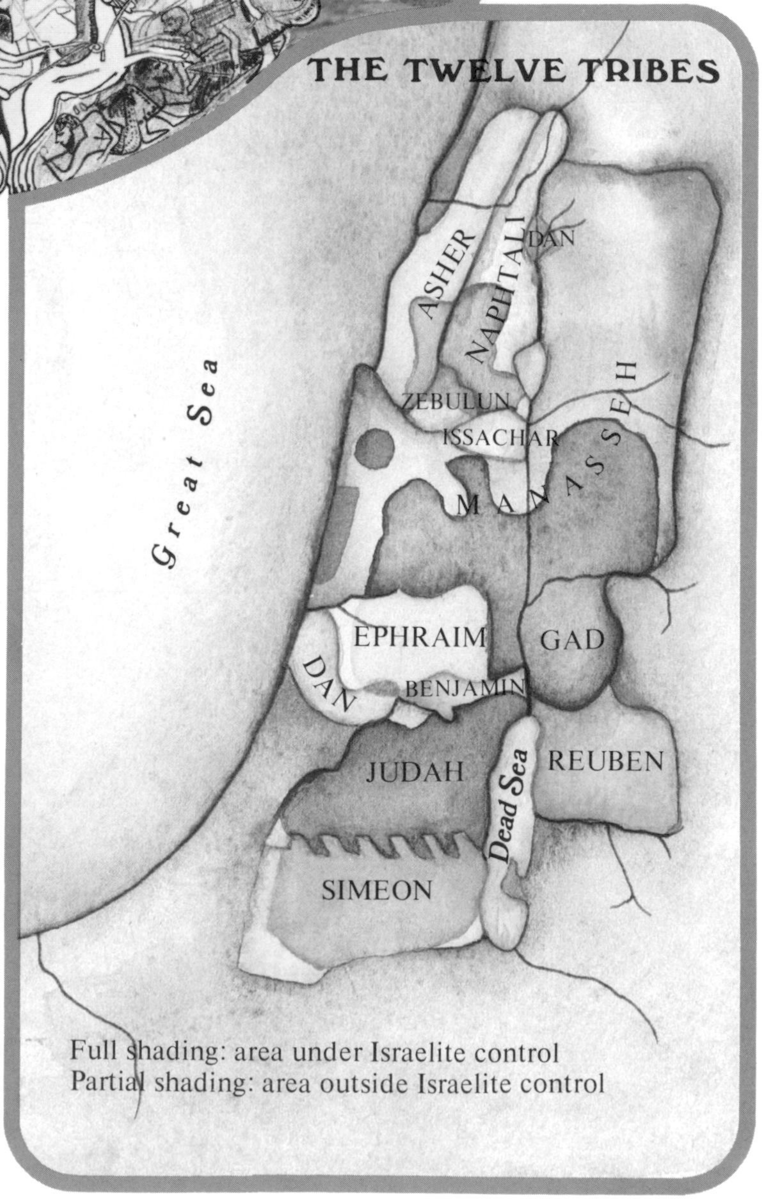

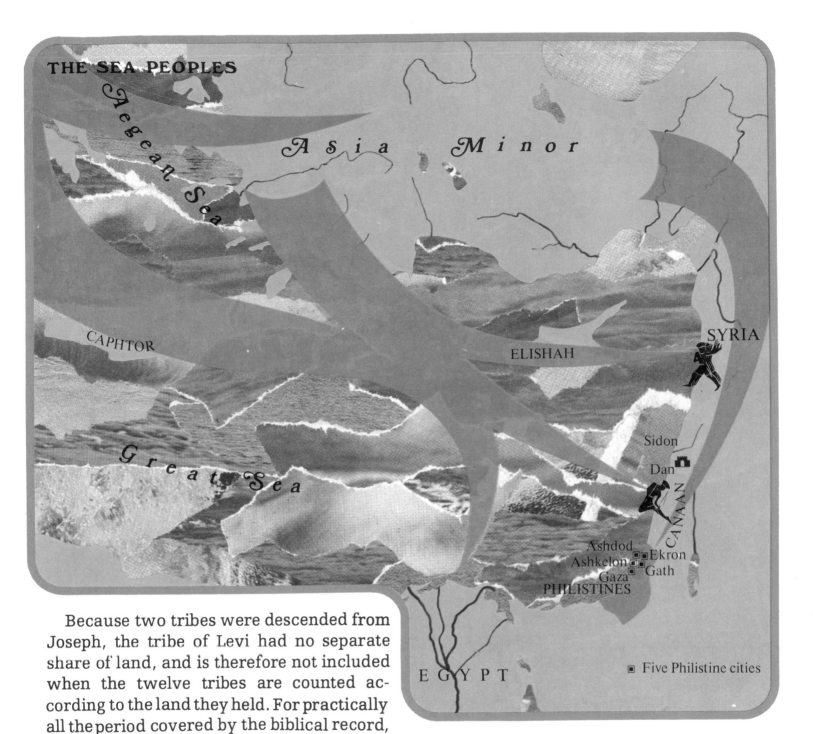

THE SEA PEOPLES

Aegean Sea

Asia Minor

CAPHTOR

ELISHAH

SYRIA

Great Sea

Sidon

Dan

CANAAN

Ashdod
Ashkelon ⊡⊡ Ekron
Gaza ⊡⊡ Gath
PHILISTINES

⊡ Five Philistine cities

EGYPT

Because two tribes were descended from Joseph, the tribe of Levi had no separate share of land, and is therefore not included when the twelve tribes are counted according to the land they held. For practically all the period covered by the biblical record, Levi was a religious tribe, from which the priests and other temple servants were drawn. The other tribes united to provide the material needs of the Levites.

The tribe of Dan originally settled to the west of Judah. But they were increasingly troubled by the Philistines who arrived in the country from the Mediterranean about the same time as the Israelites entered it from the desert. About 1200 BC a number of governments in the Aegean area collapsed and many people sailed east seeking a new home. The Egyptian kings (especially Rameses III) resisted these 'people of the sea' when they attacked the Mediterranean coast of Egypt. The Philistines, the best organized of the 'people of the sea', then landed on the coast of Canaan and settled there, establishing themselves in the five cities of Gaza, Ashkelon, Ashdod, Ekron and Gath. The Danites felt themselves so threatened that the greater part of their tribe migrated north to a new home near the sources of the Jordan. There they settled and stayed until, with other northern Israelites, they were overrun and deported by the Assyrians in 732 BC. Their principal city, Dan, had an important sanctuary and a priesthood which claimed descent from Moses.

21

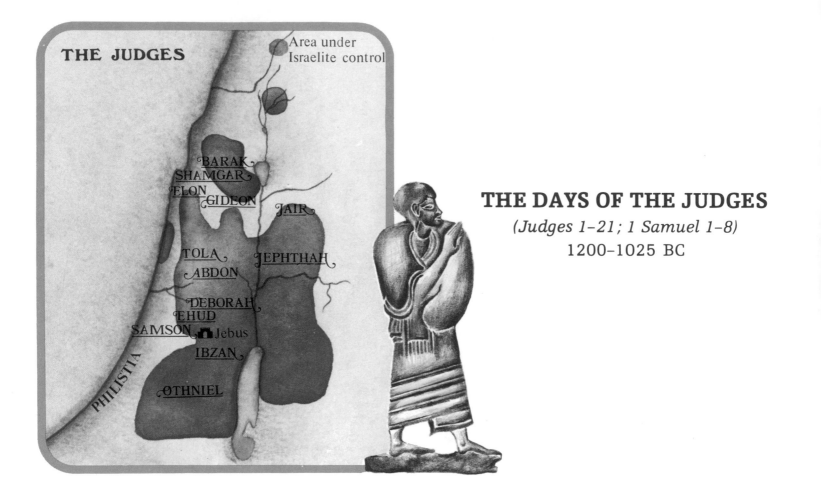

Area under
Israelite control

BARAK
SHAMGAR
ELON
GIDEON
JAIR
TOLA
ABDON
JEPHTHAH
DEBORAH
EHUD
SAMSON Jebus
IBZAN
OTHNIEL
PHILISTIA

THE DAYS OF THE JUDGES
(Judges 1–21; 1 Samuel 1–8)
1200–1025 BC

The two centuries following the Israelites' first settlement in Canaan were far from peaceful. The dispossessed Canaanites made repeated attempts to regain control of their homelands. Other armed groups made raids from Transjordan. Among these were the Israelites' own kinsfolk, the Moabites and Ammonites, who had their headquarters east of the Jordan and the Dead Sea. The fact that they were kinsfolk did not prevent them from being looked on as enemies when they invaded Israelite territory on both banks of the Jordan. Two heroes, or "judges", are remembered for their part in resisting these invaders: Ehud, the left-handed man of Benjamin, who took action against the Moabites and assassinated their king, Eglon, at Jericho, and Jephthah, the half-Israelite Transjordanian, who drove back the Ammonites.

As for the Canaanites, the military governors of the cities in the Plain of Jezreel imposed their control over the Israelite tribes north and south of the plain, and were steadily reducing them to serfdom. At last the northern and central tribes took united action against their oppressors. The first step was taken by the prophetess Deborah, who lived in the hill country of Ephraim. She ordered Barak, of the tribe of Naphtali (one of the northern tribes), to conduct a holy war against the Canaanites. The message was sent throughout the tribes, calling them "to the aid of Yahweh against the mighty". Their united rising was crowned with success. At Taanach near Megiddo, the Canaanite forces gathered under Sisera, their commander-in-chief, to crush the Israelites. A sudden downpour flooded the torrent-bed of the Kishon and put their horses and chariots (which normally made them unbeatable) out of action. The light-armed Israelites swept down on them and put them to flight. Sisera, as he fled from the battle-field, was ingloriously killed by Jael, a nomad woman in whose tent he had sought refuge.

A vivid account of the battle and what followed is given in the Song of Deborah (Judges 5),

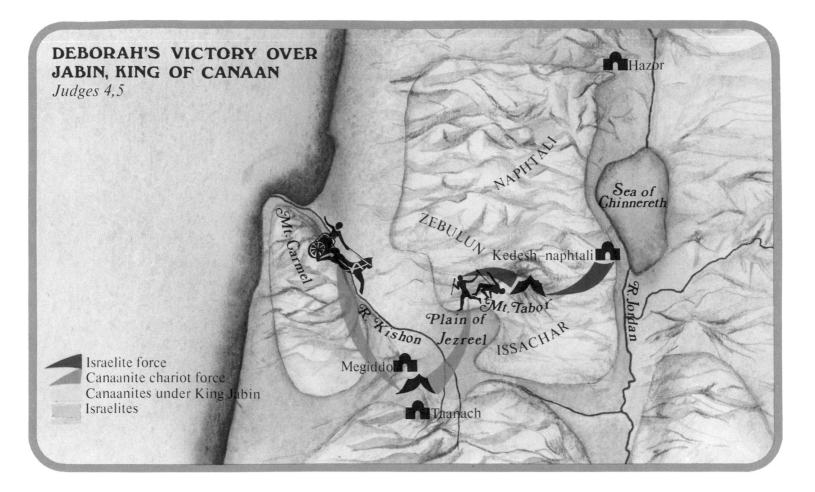

DEBORAH'S VICTORY OVER JABIN, KING OF CANAAN
Judges 4,5

Hazor

NAPHTALI

Sea of Chinnereth

ZEBULUN

Mt. Carmel

Kedesh–naphtali

Mt. Tabor

Plain of Jezreel

ISSACHAR

R. Kishon

R. Jordan

Megiddo

Taanach

Israelite force
Canaanite chariot force
Canaanites under King Jabin
Israelites

composed not long after the event it celebrates. In the song the tribes that failed to respond to the call to battle are reproached, but nothing is said of any call going to Judah; it was too isolated to be included at this time (about 1125 BC).

The next great threat came from bedouin of the eastern desert, called Midianites. Mounted on camels, they raided the Israelites' territory year by year at harvest time and destroyed their crops. The Israelites were rallied by a leader from the tribe of Manasseh, Gideon by name. He led a small mobile band against the invaders, took them by surprise, chased them across the Jordan and put an end to their raids. The grateful Israelites begged Gideon to become their king and found a hereditary monarchy, but he refused. He insisted that Yahweh alone should be acknowledged as ''king'' in Israel.

But the greatest threat to Israel as a nation in the days of the judges came from the Philistines. Having settled in the south-western coastal plain of Canaan, they intermarried with the Canaanites and soon took over the Canaanite language and religion, but maintained their political and military organization. (The land occupied by the Philistines came to be known as *Philistia*, a name which over the centuries became *Palestine*, and was given to the land of Canaan as a whole). As the Philistines extended their power from the coast into the rest of Canaan, they did not threaten the existence or the livelihood of the Israelites; they simply made them their subjects.

One means by which the Philistines were able to do this was by forbidding anyone else to work in iron. These were the early days of the Iron Age in that part of the world, but the Israelites were slow in developing the art of iron-working. The Canaanites in the Plain of Jezreel had been able to dominate them by means of Sisera's force of 900 iron-shod chariots, until the day when a heavy storm had made those chariots more of a hindrance than a help to their crews. So now the Philistines would not permit any smith to work in the Israelite territory under their control; those Israelites who had iron-shod agricultural implements had to get a Philistine smith to sharpen them. The Israelites were not allowed to have iron swords or spears.

From their five cities, then, the Philistines steadily extended their authority along the principal lines of communication. Their control of the Plain of Jezreel prevented any united action by the northern and central tribes of Israel. Yet their domination was not extraordinarily oppressive. If the Israelites were content to be subjects, they could live comfortably enough on their small farms. In the villages along the border between the areas of Philistine and Israelite occupation they existed together peacefully enough for them occasionally to intermarry.

This is plain from the story of Samson, which occupies four chapters of the book of Judges. Samson who was born at Zorah, belonged to the original territory of the tribe of Dan, some miles west of Jerusalem, on the edge of the area of Philistine settlement.

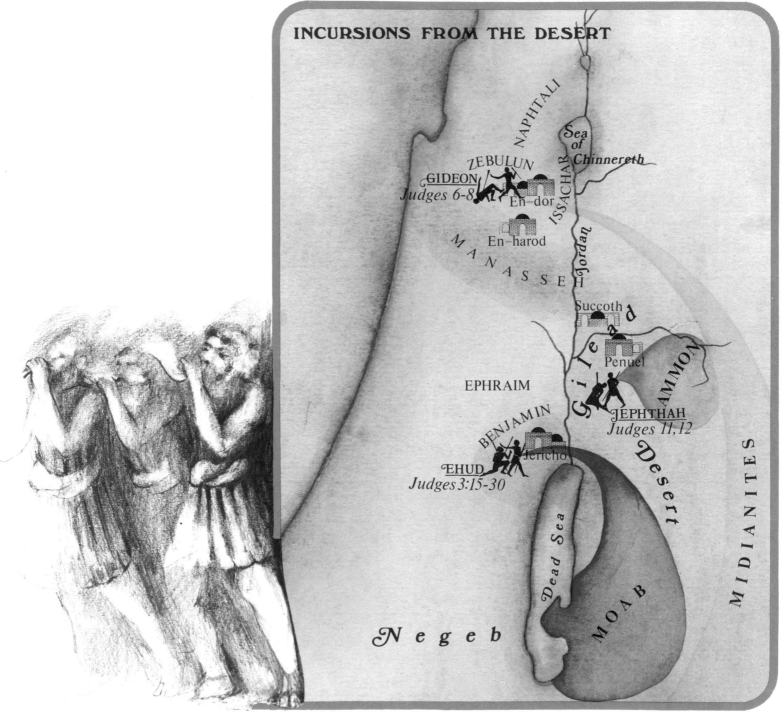

INCURSIONS FROM THE DESERT

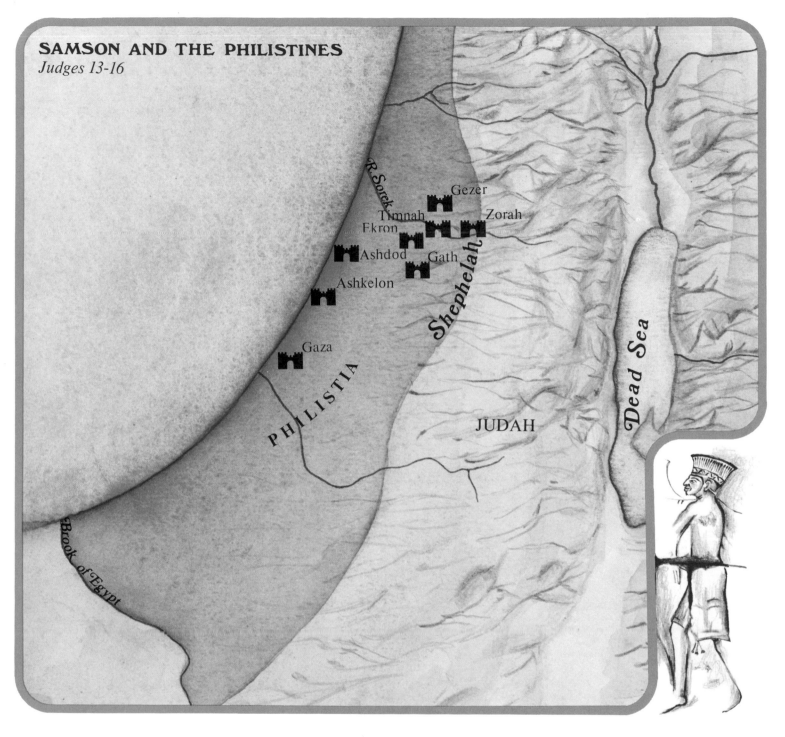

SAMSON AND THE PHILISTINES
Judges 13-16

R. Sorek

Gezer

Timnah

Zorah

Ekron

Ashdod

Gath

Ashkelon

Shephelah

Gaza

Dead Sea

PHILISTIA

JUDAH

Brook of Egypt

Samson married a Philistine girl from Timnah. His parents, old-fashioned Israelites, were rather scandalized at his proposing to do so, but they did not refuse to make the necessary arrangements with the girl's parents. Samson's single-handed exploits against the Philistines arose out of a quarrel with his wife's family, but the successive acts of revenge on either side which resulted from this dismayed the Israelite villagers. They were annoyed with Samson for stirring up trouble between them and the Philistines, and on one occasion a band of men from Judah actually handed him over bound to the Philistines. Samson escaped easily enough, but the men of Judah had shown clearly where their sympathies lay. Samson lived on in popular memory as a folk-hero, but his exploits made no more difference to the Philistine domination than those of Robin Hood to the Norman Conquest in England.

The centre of Israel's religious life at this time was Shiloh, in Ephraimite territory, where the ark of the covenant, the symbol of Yahweh's presence among his people, was housed. The priestly family in charge of this inter-tribal sanctuary traced its descent from

Aaron, Moses' brother. The last of the chief priests of Shiloh was Eli, who was more than a priest; he "judged" Israel in the sense that he was called upon to settle inter-tribal disputes.

In Eli's days the central tribes of Israel decided to rebel against their Philistine overlords. They came to Shiloh to receive the priestly blessing on their scheme, and made sure of success (as they imagined) by having the sacred ark itself carried into battle at their head. But they were defeated at Aphek, some 12 miles east of Joppa; the ark was captured by the Philistines and Eli's two sons, Hophni and Phinehas, who were in attendance on it, were killed. Eli himself died on receiving the news of the disaster, and Shiloh itself, with its sanctuary, was probably destroyed at that time. It did indeed appear that the glory had departed from Israel for ever.

That the glory did not depart was due to one man – the prophet Samuel. He had become the centre of the nation's life, acting not only as prophet but as judge and priest also. The

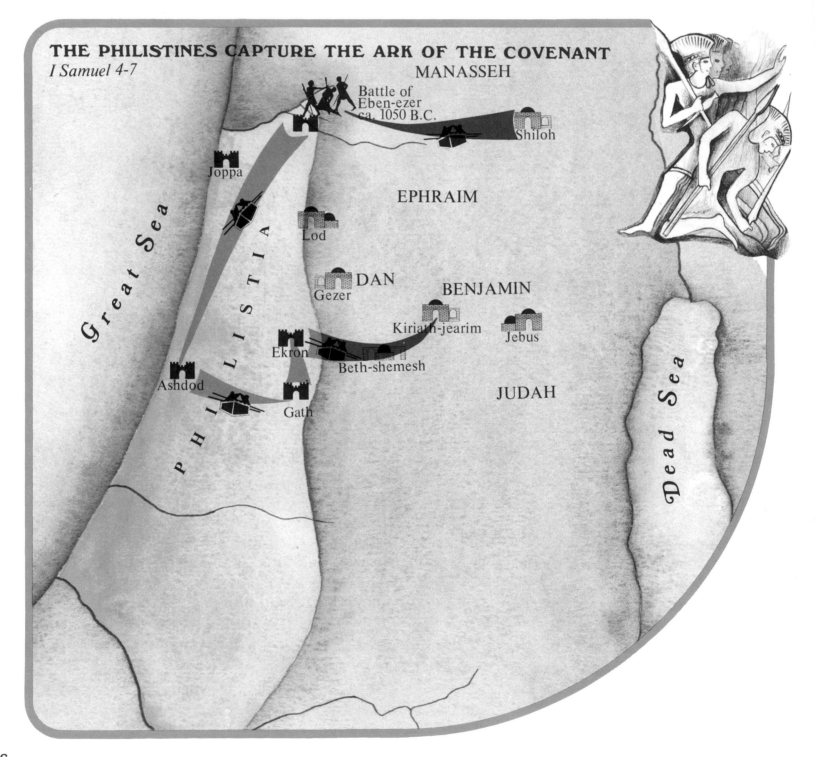

THE PHILISTINES CAPTURE THE ARK OF THE COVENANT
I Samuel 4-7

MANASSEH

Battle of
Eben-ezer
ca. 1050 B.C.

Shiloh

Joppa

EPHRAIM

Lod

Great Sea

DAN

BENJAMIN

Gezer

Kiriath-jearim

Jebus

Ekron

Beth-shemesh

Ashdod

JUDAH

Gath

PHILISTIA

Dead Sea

time came when the Philistines, who had found the ark too hot to hold, and had passed it from one city to another, restored it to Israel. But Samuel deliberately allowed it to be kept hidden in a private house at Kiriath-jearim, 8 miles west of Jerusalem. The people had come to regard it superstitiously as a lucky charm, and it had let them down. Samuel would teach them to place their trust in Yahweh alone. In place of Shiloh, four places were chosen to which Samuel went in turn to pronounce judgment and offer sacrifice – Mizpah, Gilgal, Bethel and his own homestead at Ramah in Ephraim. Under his wise and patient guidance the people returned to their true covenant-loyalty and recovered their national self-respect. The time came when they took the field once more against the Philistines and, on the very ground where they had suffered such a disastrous defeat, they put the Philistines to flight so effectively (aided by a thunderstorm which threw the enemy into confusion) that for several years the central highlands were left in peace.

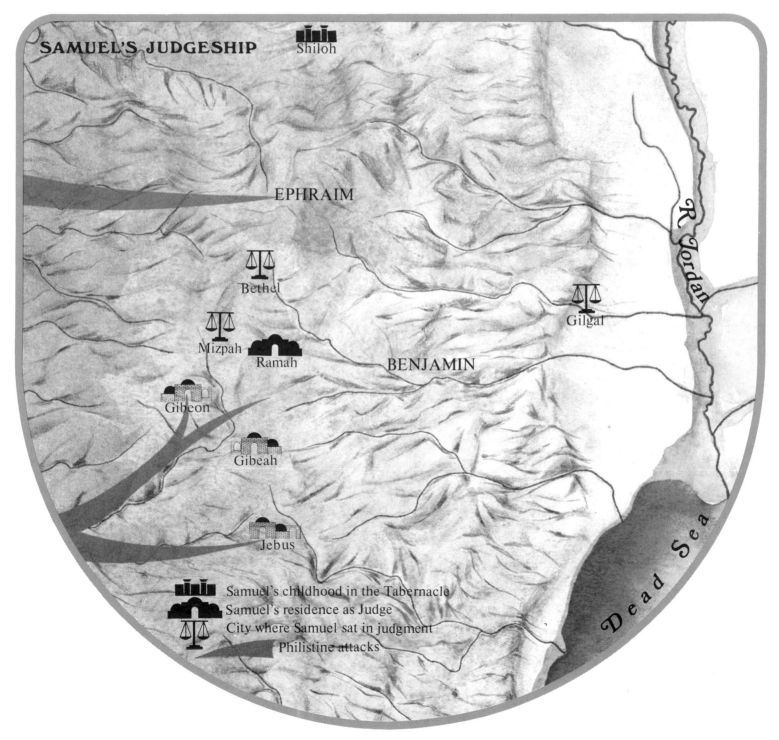

SAMUEL'S JUDGESHIP

Shiloh

EPHRAIM

Bethel

Gilgal

Mizpah

Ramah

BENJAMIN

Gibeon

Gibeah

Jebus

Samuel's childhood in the Tabernacle
Samuel's residence as Judge
City where Samuel sat in judgment
Philistine attacks

R. Jordan

Dead Sea

THE KINGDOM OF SAUL

(I Samuel 8–31)

1025–1010 BC

Samuel's leadership was unrivalled, but he had no obvious successor. As judges, his sons were unacceptable to the people. They were suspected of taking bribes and giving decisions in favour of those who paid them best.

The people decided that what they needed was a king, to rule them justly and lead them in battle. The surrounding nations had their kings: why should they not have one? They approached Samuel, therefore, and asked him to appoint a king. Samuel was not greatly pleased at what appeared to be a lack of confidence in himself, but when they persisted, he named a man of Benjamin called Saul, who lived at Gibeah, a few miles north of Jerusalem. Saul's most obvious qualification for the honour was his height: he was head and shoulders above other people. Many were inclined to despise him as a mere nobody. But just then Saul had an opportunity of showing his real worth.

Across the Jordan was the settlement of Jabesh-gilead, closely related by blood to Saul's own tribe of Benjamin. The people of Jabesh-gilead were threatened by the king of Ammon, who ruled the territory to the south of them. When they sought terms, he contemptuously allowed them seven days to find effective help against him; otherwise they would have to endure humiliation and slavery. When their urgent appeal for help reached Gibeah, Saul sent a summons to united action throughout the tribes of Israel and arrived to give help to Jabesh-gilead in an amazingly short space of time. The Ammonites were beaten off, Jabesh-gilead was delivered, and Saul was the hero of the hour. The people assembled at Mizpah in the central highlands to acclaim him as their king, anointed and chosen by Yahweh.

In addition to this, Yahweh's approval of Saul's appointment as king seemed to be assured when Saul suddenly showed the gift of prophecy. This was a surprise to everybody, as he had given no signs previously of being what is called a "charismatic" person. This occurrence, we are told, gave rise to a proverbial saying: "Is Saul also among the prophets?" A man might have the gifts necessary for being a wise judge and a successful general, but only God could make a prophet.

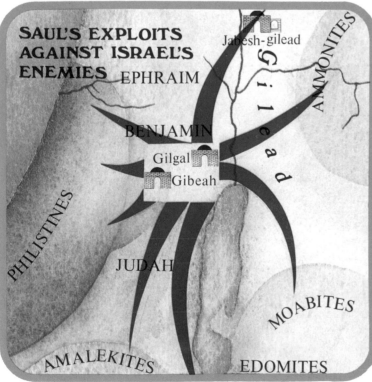

But Saul's gift of prophecy might bring him into conflict with Samuel, who was first and foremost a prophet. Samuel had not given up his moral and religious authority. If Saul were content to exercise his kingship as supreme judge and military leader, and allow Samuel to continue his priestly and prophetic ministry, the combination might be a blessing to Israel. But that was not to be.

It was the Philistine danger, however, that chiefly lay behind the people's demand for a king. Jonathan, Saul's eldest son, took matters into his own hands by killing the Philistine prefect at Geba, not far from his father's headquarters at Gibeah. Reprisals followed: a Philistine band established itself at Michmash, at a point where they could cut the lines of communication between Benjamin and the more powerful tribe of Ephraim and then destroy the divided Israelite forces. Saul's army consisted of peasant volunteers, who saw with dismay the plight they were in and began quietly to melt away.

At this point Jonathan, who was so largely responsible for this critical situation, resolved it by a daring commando type move. Accompanied by his armour-bearer, he climbed up the rock of Michmash by the steepest route. The Philistine garrison thought that a considerable band of Israelites was coming against them, and came out to deal with them. Jonathan and his companion stationed themselves at a narrow point where only one man could pass at a time between two rocks, and picked off the Philistines one by one. The garrison panicked. Saul's scouts, looking from Gibeah north to Michmash, saw the signs of panic. Saul consulted the sacred oracle, learned from the priest in charge of it that the time was suitable for an attack, and inflicted great slaughter on the Philistines. Their hold on

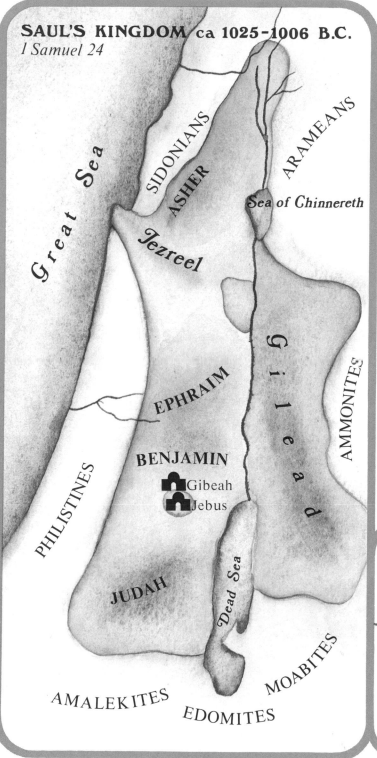

SAUL'S KINGDOM ca 1025–1006 B.C.
1 Samuel 24

Great Sea

SIDONIANS

ASHER

ARAMEANS

Sea of Chinnereth

Jezreel

EPHRAIM

Gilead

AMMONITES

BENJAMIN

Gibeah

Jebus

PHILISTINES

Dead Sea

JUDAH

AMALEKITES

EDOMITES

MOABITES

DAVID AND GOLIATH
1 Samuel 17

DAVID

Azekah

GOLIATH

Gath

Socoh

PHILISTIA

JUDAH

central Canaan was broken for the time being.

Saul's military success was spoiled, however, by the growing conflict between himself and Samuel. The conflict began when Saul offered sacrifice before a battle, because Samuel was late in arriving. It was made worse when, during the period

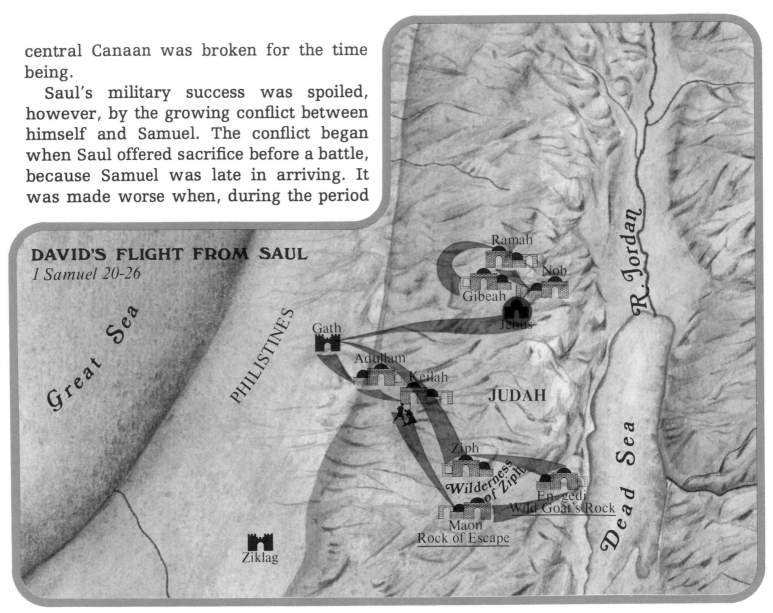

DAVID'S FLIGHT FROM SAUL
1 Samuel 20-26

of peace won by the defeat of the Philistines at Michmash, Samuel ordered Saul to wipe out the Amalekites. The Amalekites were a group living in the Negeb, with whom the Israelites had a perpetual blood-feud because the Amalekites had launched an unprovoked attack on them in the days of their wilderness wanderings. Saul was quite willing to wipe out the Amalekites, but he saw no reason to wipe out their flocks and herds; these could increase the wealth of himself and his followers. Moreover, as a king, Saul appreciated the dignity of kingship, so he spared the Amalekite king Agag. Samuel met him on his return from this expedition and announced that, because of his disobedience, God had deprived him of the kingship and would give it to someone else.

The someone else whom Samuel had in mind was David, a young man from Bethlehem in Judah, whom Saul promoted to high honour because of the energy with which he took action against the Philistines. Indeed, after he had killed the Philistine champion, Goliath, David became the king's son-in-law. But Saul came to suspect that David was the man whom Samuel intended to take his place, and after one or two attempts by Saul on his life, David left the royal service and became the leader of a band of outlawed men in the Negeb. In due course he offered the services of his men and himself as mercenaries in the army of Achish, king of Gath.

Saul was a deeply religious man, and herein lies his tragedy. A less religious man would have ignored Samuel's protests, and might even have silenced them. But to Saul Samuel was still the mouthpiece of God, and the thought that he had offended God preyed on

Saul's mind, so that he became depressed and imagined that everyone was against him.

For all this, he did not forget his kingly duties. Having brought central Canaan under his control, he turned his attention to the south. The tribal territory of Judah was David's homeland. To establish his power in Judah and the Negeb, Saul judged it necessary to clear out David and his followers, in whom he now saw dangerous rivals. He pursued them from place to place and when David was betrayed at the town of Ziph, he and his men were forced to cross over into Philistine territory.

It remained for Saul to bring the northern tribes into the unity of Israel. The Philistines' hold on the plain of Jezreel had to be broken, so Saul led an army north to give them battle. The Philistines assembled in Aphek and from there marched to Shunem, where they set up camps. Battle was joined at Mount Gilboa, on the southern edge of the plain, and it ended in disaster for the Israelites. Saul was killed, and so were Jonathan and two of his brothers. The Philistines took their revenge by mutilating their bodies and fastening them to the wall of the temple of Dagon in Beth-shean. But the men of Jabesh-gilead, remembering how Saul had saved them from the Ammonites, crossed the Jordan by night, removed the bodies and carried them back home, to give them decent burial there.

It looked as if the Philistine grip on the whole land of Israel was firmer than ever. Saul had made a valiant attempt to break it, but he had failed. Yet, if Saul had not made the attempt, his successor might not have succeeded where Saul failed.

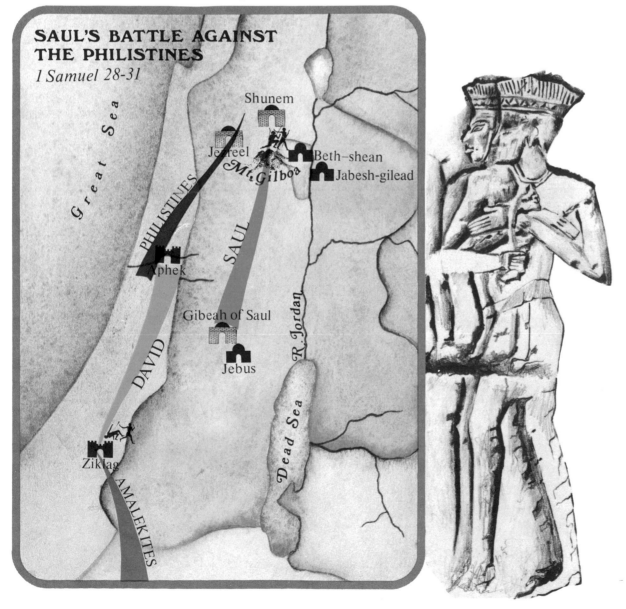

SAUL'S BATTLE AGAINST THE PHILISTINES
1 Samuel 28-31

Great Sea

Shunem

Jezreel • Beth-shean

Mt. Gilboa • Jabesh-gilead

PHILISTINES

SAUL

R. Jordan

Aphek

Gibeah of Saul

DAVID

Jebus

Dead Sea

Ziklag

AMALEKITES

THE KINGDOM OF DAVID

(2 Samuel 1–24; 1 Kings 1–2)

1010–970 BC

A few of Saul's followers escaped across the Jordan, and there, at Mahanaim, they set up his surviving son Eshbaal as king of Israel. Eshbaal was a weakling, but he was fortunate in having his uncle Abner, an experienced soldier, as his commander.

News of Saul's death reached David in Ziklag, a small city in the Negeb where the king of Gath had allowed him and his followers to live. On hearing the news, he consulted the oracle of Yahweh and was directed to go to Hebron, the principal city of Judah. Here he was met by the elders of the tribe of Judah who made him their king. The Philistines saw no objection in this: David (they thought) would be their loyal subject. As they expected, fighting broke out between the followers of Eshbaal and David, and this (they hoped) would weaken both sides.

In one of the battles between the two sides – at Gibeon, north of Jebus (Jerusalem) – Abner killed a cousin of David named Asahel. Asahel was the younger brother of Joab, David's commander-in-chief, and Joab swore revenge for his brother's death. Not long

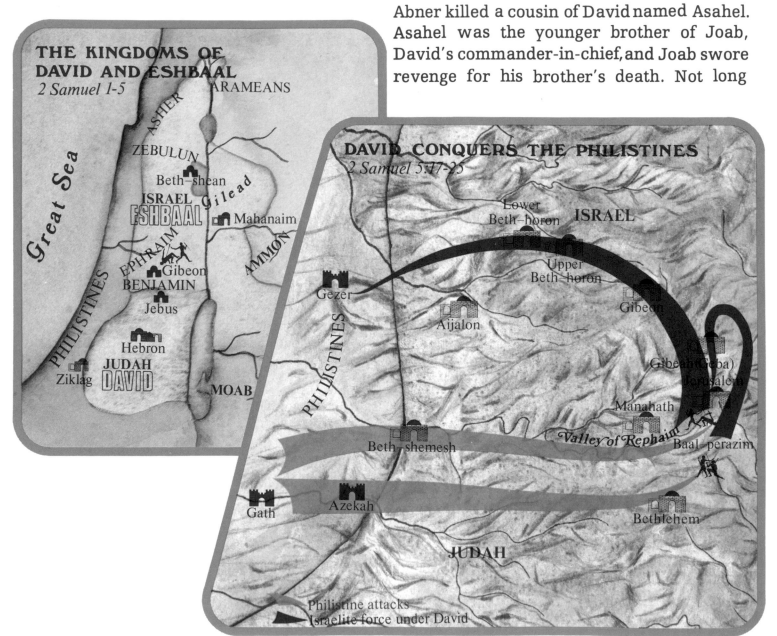

THE KINGDOMS OF DAVID AND ESHBAAL
2 Samuel 1–5

ARAMEANS

ASHER

ZEBULUN

Beth-shean

ISRAEL
ESHBAAL

Gilead

Mahanaim

Great Sea

EPHRAIM

Gibeon

BENJAMIN

Jebus

AMMON

PHILISTINES

Hebron

JUDAH
DAVID

Ziklag

MOAB

DAVID CONQUERS THE PHILISTINES
2 Samuel 5:17–25

Lower Beth-horon   ISRAEL

Upper Beth-horon

Gezer

Gibeon

Aijalon

PHILISTINES

Gibeah (Geba)

Jerusalem

Manahath

Valley of Rephaim

Baal-perazim

Beth-shemesh

Gath   Azekah

Bethlehem

JUDAH

Philistine attacks
Israelite force under David

32

afterwards, Abner quarrelled with Eshbaal and went over to David's side. David gave him a warm welcome, but Joab seized the first opportunity of assassinating him, to David's great embarrassment.

Abner's action meant the collapse of Eshbaal's cause. Two of Eshbaal's courtiers murdered him, foolishly thinking that by so doing they would win David's favour. Instead, when they brought him Eshbaal's head, he put them to death as criminals. Representatives of all the tribes (now leaderless) came to David at Hebron and begged him to be their king. David consented, and entered into a covenant with them.

David's new rank, as king of Judah and Israel, was not to the liking of the Philistines. He must be put down before he grew more powerful. They marched against David. David withdrew to his old base at Adullam (where he had collected his followers in the reign of Saul) and from there he made a surprise attack on the Philistines as they advanced on Hebron, defeating them first at the Valley of Rephaim, west of Jerusalem. He followed up this first defeat with a second one in the same region, pursuing the enemy from Geba to Gezer. From this they never recovered. Before long it was the Philistines who were David's subjects.

Having broken the power of the Philistines, David moved against Jerusalem, which had remained in Canaanite(Jebusite) hands since Israel's entry into the country. Jerusalem stood on the ridge of Ophel, south of the present Old City; it was situated on top of a hill and surrounded by strongly fortified walls. But Joab, David's commander-in-chief, succeeded in taking it. The description of his doing so is not all that clear, but he appears to have led a party of men up a water-channel which led into the heart of the city. Before the

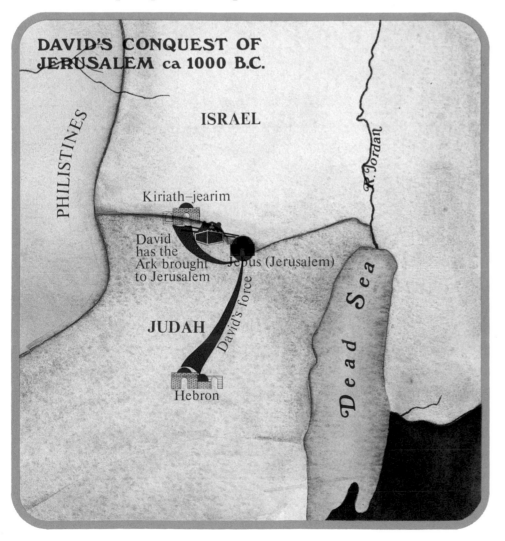

DAVID'S CONQUEST OF JERUSALEM ca 1000 B.C.

PHILISTINES

ISRAEL

R. Jordan

Kiriath–jearim

David has the Ark brought to Jerusalem

Jebus (Jerusalem)

David's force

JUDAH

Dead Sea

Hebron

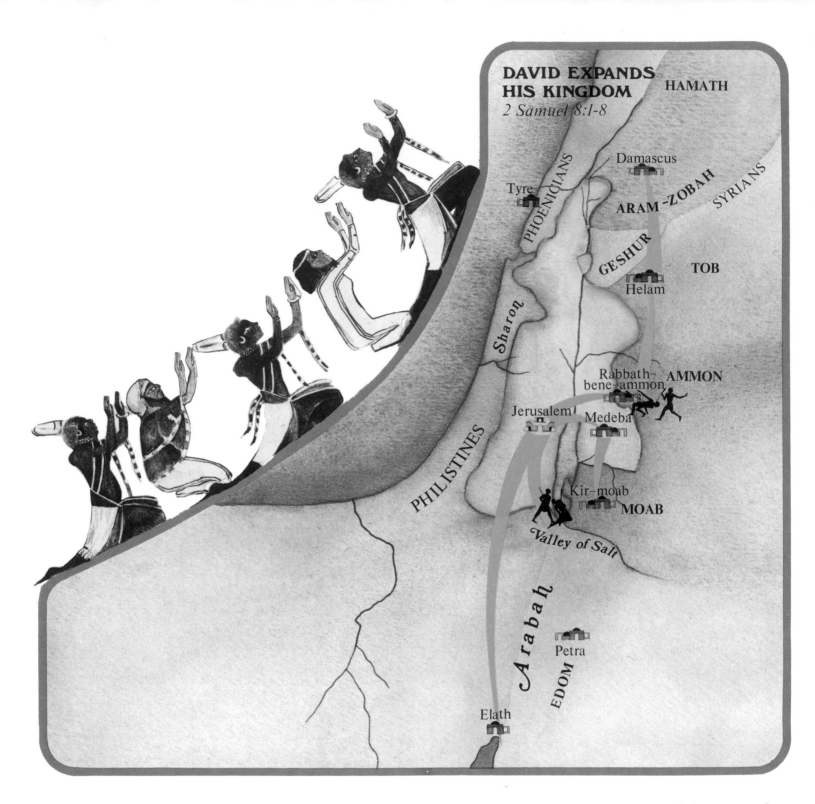

DAVID EXPANDS HIS KINGDOM
2 Samuel 8:1-8

HAMATH

Damascus

Tyre

PHOENICIANS

ARAM-ZOBAH

SYRIANS

GESHUR

TOB

Helam

Sharon

Rabbath-bene-ammon

AMMON

Jerusalem

Medeba

PHILISTINES

Kir-moab

MOAB

Valley of Salt

Arabah

Petra

EDOM

Elath

inhabitants realized what had happened, the enemy were in their midst, and in control.

The capture of Jerusalem, in the seventh year of his reign, was of great importance for David. Here he had an ideal capital. It belonged neither to Israel nor to Judah, so neither of his kingdoms could complain that he had favoured the other in his choice of a capital. It was in a good position to withstand attack. Its religious importance went back to ancient times: this was Salem, royal city of Melchizedek, priest of God Most High, who received tithes from Abraham and bestowed his blessing on him. But David increased its religious significance by bringing the ark of God from its long retirement in Kiriath-jearim and placing it in a tent-shrine on Mount Zion, on the north side of his new capital. Jerusalem thus became the central sanctuary for all Israel and Judah – the place which Yahweh their God had chosen to be the dwelling-place for his name (as it is put in the book of Deuteronomy).

For the first time in its history, the land of Israel was now under united control. At this time the great Near Eastern powers were weakened, and David took advantage of this to build an empire for himself, by war and diplomacy, until his influence stretched from the Egyptian border to the Upper Euphrates.

The conquest of Edom made David master of the territory between the Dead Sea and Elath, on the Gulf of Aqaba. Sela or Petra, its rock-capital, fell into his hands. Moab, east of the Dead Sea, was added to his empire, so was Ammon, farther north. The whole of Transjordan was now under David's control.

David then turned his attention to his northern neighbours. The king of Zobah, north of Damascus, had helped the Ammonites. This was as good a reason as any to make war against him, and the king of Zobah was overthrown. Damascus had aided him against David, so Damascus was also forced to surrender to David's rule. David placed military garrisons in Damascus and other Aramean cities. Further north lay the Hittite kingdom of Hamath. Its king made haste to send an embassy to David and in effect became subject to him.

David also entered into an alliance with Hiram, king of Tyre and overlord of Phoenicia. This was an economic alliance, bringing benefits to both sides. Hiram could import grain from the fertile parts of David's kingdom and other goods through the Red Sea port of Elath. David gained a share in the proceeds of Phoenician sea trade, and hired Phoenician architects to make Jerusalem a worthy capital for a great empire.

The later part of David's reign was troubled by a succession of revolts. The most serious was led by his favourite son Absalom, who was able to detach the loyalty of many of the people of Judah from

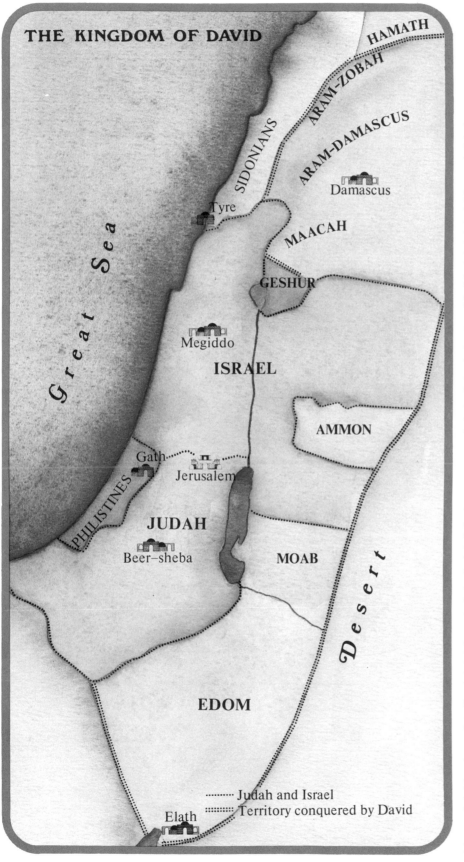

THE KINGDOM OF DAVID

HAMATH

ARAM-ZOBAH

SIDONIANS

ARAM-DAMASCUS

Damascus

Tyre

MAACAH

GESHUR

Great Sea

Megiddo

ISRAEL

AMMON

Gath

Jerusalem

JUDAH

PHILISTINES

Beer-sheba

MOAB

Desert

EDOM

········ Judah and Israel
:::::::: Territory conquered by David

Elath

his father. David and his faithful followers escaped to Transjordan: when Absalom pursued them there, he was caught and killed by Joab, and the army which he had led against David melted away.

Then it was the turn of the men of Israel to revolt. They perhaps felt that David had not been sufficiently grateful to them for remaining loyal during Absalom's revolt. They found a leader in a man named Sheba, who proclaimed that David's Judean dynasty had no longer any authority over Israel. Once again it was Joab who put down this rebellion leading his army as far north as Abel-beth-maacah. Joab was not over careful about the methods he used, but David had good reason to be grateful for Joab's loyalty and military ability.

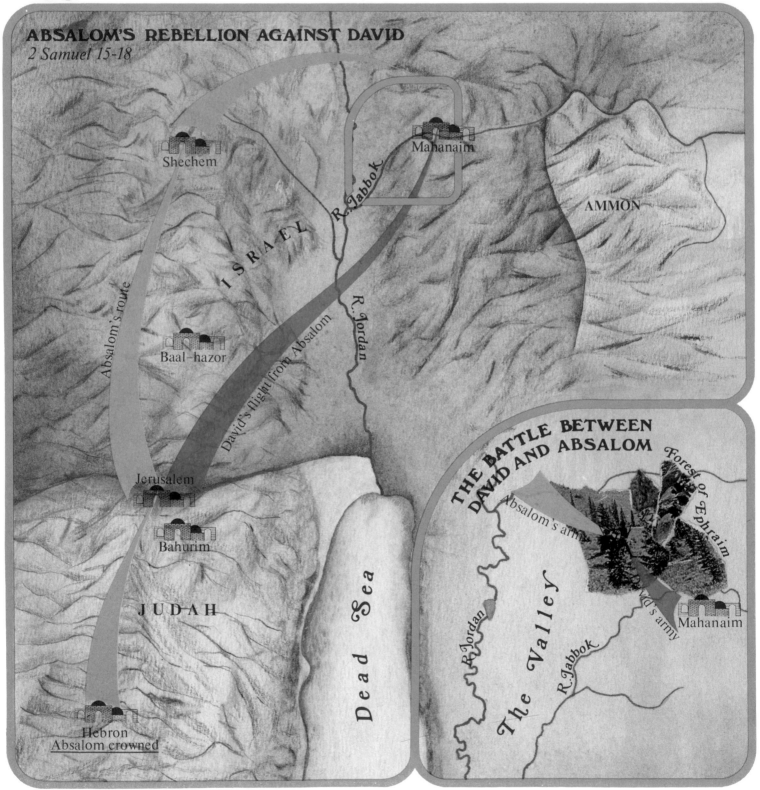

ABSALOM'S REBELLION AGAINST DAVID
2 Samuel 15-18

Shechem

Mahanaim

AMMON

I S R A E L

R. Jabbok

Absalom's route

R. Jordan

David's flight from Absalom

Baal-hazor

Jerusalem

Bahurim

Dead Sea

J U D A H

Hebron
Absalom crowned

THE BATTLE BETWEEN DAVID AND ABSALOM

Forest of Ephraim

Absalom's army

David's army

Mahanaim

R. Jordan

R. Jabbok

The Valley

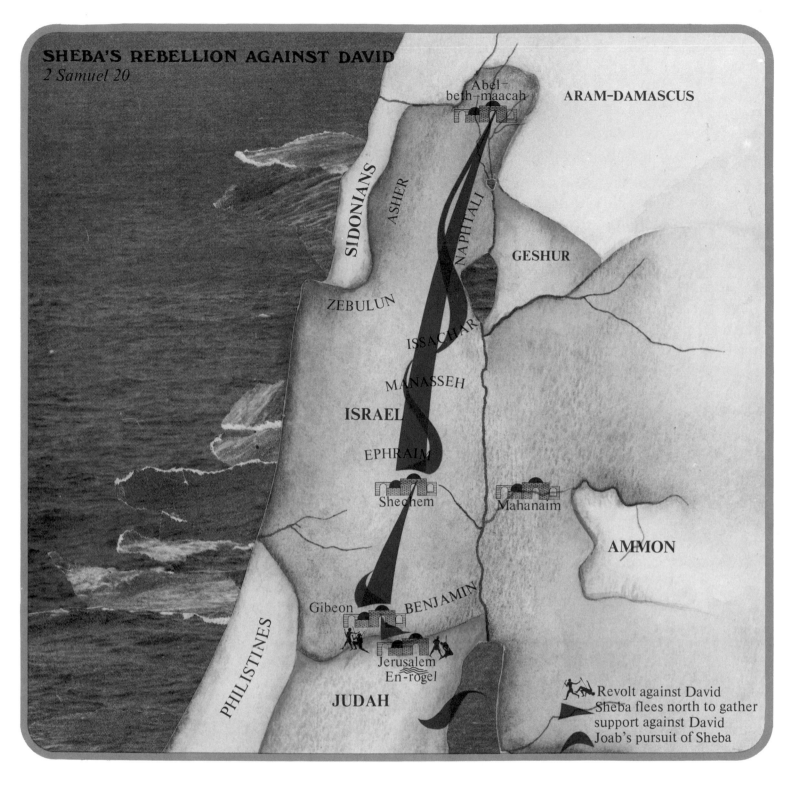

SHEBA'S REBELLION AGAINST DAVID
2 Samuel 20

ARAM-DAMASCUS

Abel-beth-maacah

SIDONIANS

ASHER

NAPHTALI

GESHUR

ZEBULUN

ISSACHAR

MANASSEH

ISRAEL

EPHRAIM

Shechem

Mahanaim

AMMON

Gibeon

BENJAMIN

PHILISTINES

Jerusalem
En-rogel

JUDAH

Revolt against David
Sheba flees north to gather
support against David
Joab's pursuit of Sheba

The last revolt of David's reign was not directed against himself, but against his young son Solomon, whom he had chosen as his successor. Solomon was acceptable to the people of Jerusalem, for he was a native of their city, as was his mother Bathsheba. But some of David's old companions, including Joab and the priest Abiathar, who had shared his exile during Saul's reign, thought that David's eldest surviving son, Adonijah, ought to be king in his father's place. Accordingly they proclaimed him king at En-rogel, in the valley southeast of Jerusalem. But when news of this came to Solomon's mother, she immediately told David, who gave orders that Solomon, mounted on the king's mule, should be escorted by the royal bodyguard to the spring Gihon in the Kidron valley, and solemnly anointed king there. The fact that Solomon had the support of the royal bodyguard settled things. Those who were attending the rival festivities at En-rogel broke up in haste and went quietly home. David died in the knowledge that the son whom he had chosen would succeed him.

THE REIGN OF SOLOMON

(1 Kings 2–11)

970–930 BC

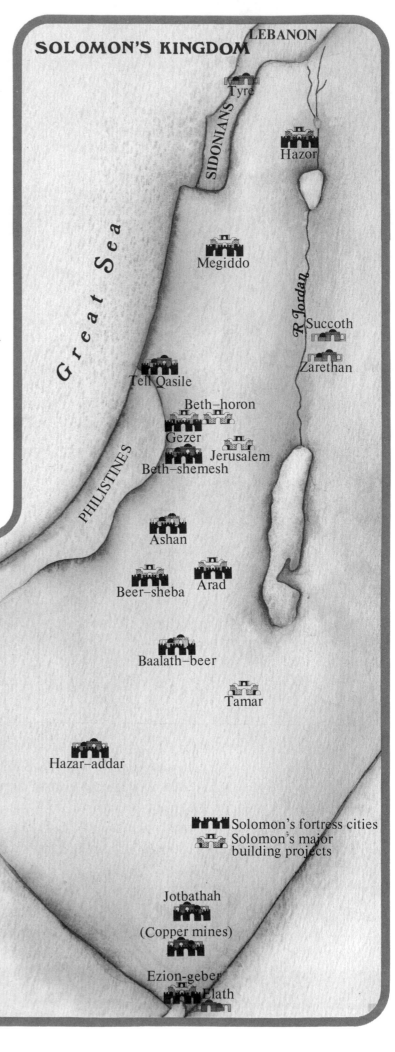

Solomon's reign had not well begun before he got rid of Adonijah and his supporters. Solomon inherited the empire which his father had acquired, and used its wealth to live far more grandly than David. He gathered a large harem, consisting mainly of the daughters of neighbouring rulers with whom he made political and economic treaties. He began a huge building programme, partly for defence, partly for business, and partly for show. It included a new royal palace, a separate palace for his queen (daughter to one of the weak Pharaohs of the twenty-first dynasty), the "hall of pillars" or assembly room, the throne-room of justice, and a treasury or armoury, called "the house of the forest of Lebanon" probably because it was panelled in cedar.

SOLOMON'S KINGDOM

LEBANON

SIDONIANS

Tyre

Hazor

Great Sea

Megiddo

R Jordan

Succoth

Zarethan

Tell Qasile

Beth-horon

Gezer

Jerusalem

Beth-shemesh

PHILISTINES

Ashan

Beer-sheba

Arad

Baalath-beer

Tamar

Hazar-addar

Solomon's fortress cities

Solomon's major building projects

Jotbathah

(Copper mines)

Ezion-geber

Elath

38

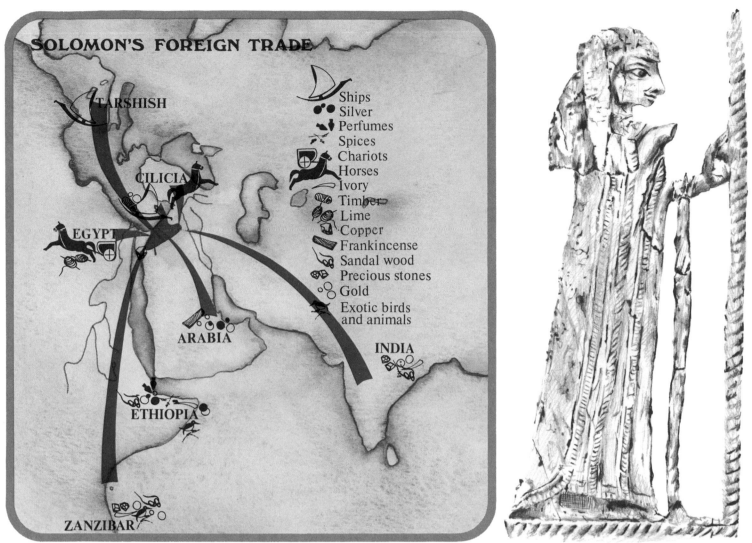

SOLOMON'S FOREIGN TRADE

Ships
Silver
Perfumes
Spices
Chariots
Horses
Ivory
Timber
Lime
Copper
Frankincense
Sandal wood
Precious stones
Gold
Exotic birds and animals

TARSHISH
CILICIA
EGYPT
ARABIA
INDIA
ETHIOPIA
ZANZIBAR

Most imposing was the temple which he built for Yahweh, north of his citadel, in the area where the Dome of the Rock and the el-Aqsa mosque now stand. Here was a natural rock-altar where, according to later tradition, Abraham prepared to sacrifice his son Isaac. Now sacrifices were to be offered to Yahweh there for a full thousand years, with two interruptions – one of about 50 years in the sixth century BC (after the destruction of Solomon's temple by Nebuchadrezzar's army) and one of three years in the second century BC (when the place was turned over to pagan worship by Antiochus Epiphanes).

To carry out this programme, Solomon hired architects and other workmen from his father's ally, Hiram, king of Tyre. As a result, he fell heavily into debt and had to mortgage some of his territory to Hiram.

Solomon increased his wealth by seaborne trade, in which Hiram allowed him to have a share; in addition, he demanded a tax on goods transported through his kingdom. Some came from Asia Minor to Egypt. Others came through Elath for Phoenicia. The goods from Asia Minor included horses, and Solomon built up a large force of horses and chariots for himself.

Considerable as Solomon's income was, it was not sufficient to maintain his expensive establishment and building projects. His subjects were more and more heavily taxed, and even compelled to provide forced labour. At first only non-Israelites were required to give this service, but later even Israelites had to give him one month's free labour out of every three. This did more than anything else to turn the tribes of Israel against the house of David: it was regarded as a breach of Yahweh's covenant by which king and people alike were bound. The kingdom was divided into twelve administrative regions, each of which was responsible to supply the court with food one month in the year.

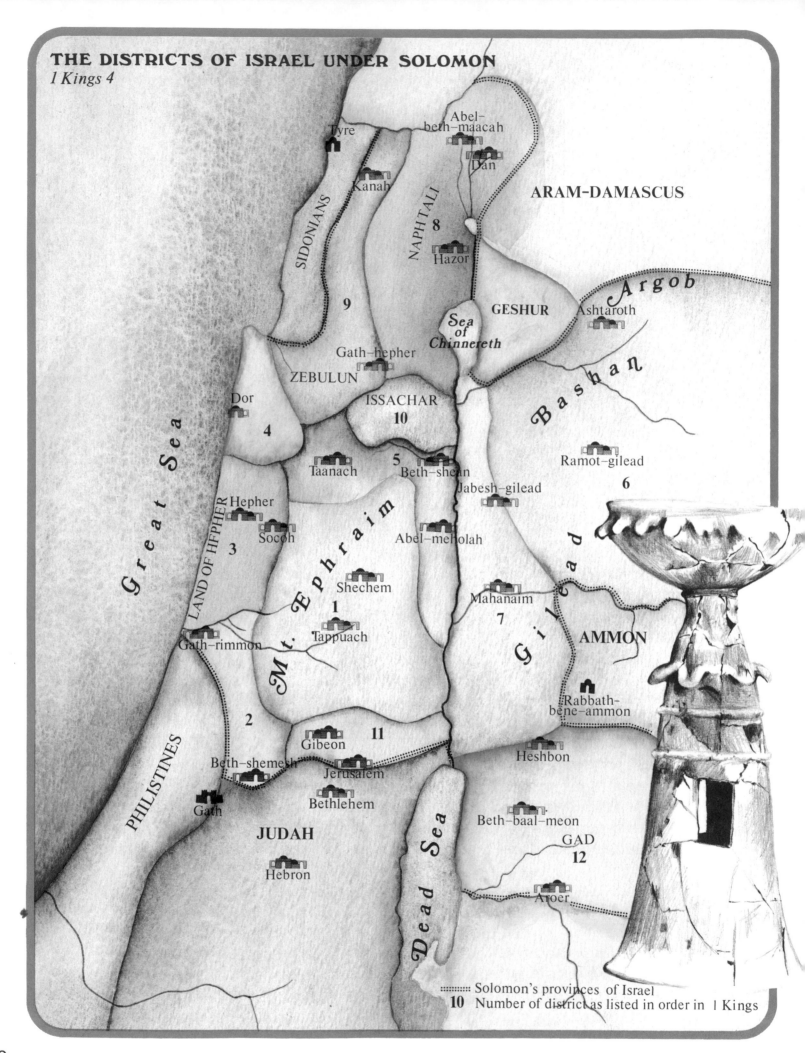

THE DISTRICTS OF ISRAEL UNDER SOLOMON
1 Kings 4

Tyre

Abel-beth-maacah

Dan

ARAM-DAMASCUS

SIDONIANS

Kanah

NAPHTALI

8

Hazor

Argob

GESHUR

Ashtaroth

9

Sea of Chinnereth

Bashan

Gath-hepher

ZEBULUN

Dor

ISSACHAR

10

4

Taanach

5

Beth-shean

Jabesh-gilead

Ramot-gilead

6

Hepher

Socoh

Abel-meholah

LAND OF HEPHER

3

Great Sea

Mt. Ephraim

Shechem

1

Mahanaim

Gilead

7

AMMON

Gath-rimmon

Tappuach

2

Rabbath-bene-ammon

11

Gibeon

Beth-shemesh

Jerusalem

Heshbon

Gath

Bethlehem

PHILISTINES

JUDAH

Dead Sea

Beth-baal-meon

GAD

12

Hebron

Aroer

.... Solomon's provinces of Israel

10   Number of district as listed in order in 1 Kings

40

Solomon's subjects did indeed enjoy the blessings of peace throughout his reign, and in later generations, when Israel and Judah had to endure hard times, the people remembered only how peace and prosperity were maintained by a king of Israel who ruled from the Egyptian frontier to the Euphrates. On this memory they based their hopes of a golden age to come. The king who would reign in this golden age was pictured as combining the military genius of David and the arts of peace associated with Solomon.

Among these arts of peace were such literary forms as the national epic and the court chronicle. The writers were Israelite, even if architects had to be brought from Phoenicia. Solomon's reign was noted also for the growth of "wisdom", for which the king himself became famous in later ages: "he uttered three thousand proverbs", we are told, "and his songs were a thousand and five." His widespread knowledge of the world of nature won him fame not only among his immediate neighbours but among more distant peoples: we recall how the caravan of the queen of Sheba came all the way from Yemen to hear the wisdom of Solomon.

Towards the end of Solomon's reign there was a change of dynasty in Egypt. Shishak, who founded the new dynasty, planned to extend his dominion into Asia. Solomon's kingdom presented a barrier to his plans, so long as it remained strong and united. Shishak therefore set himself to weaken it.

Early in Solomon's reign a former officer of the kingdom of Zobah, which David had defeated, led an independence movement which made Damascus its headquarters. This man, Rezon by name, would naturally be encouraged by Shishak. Before long, he was able to break loose from Solomon's control, and founded a dynasty which endured in Damascus for two centuries.

When David, early in his reign, conquered Edom, an infant prince of Edom, Hadad, was carried to Egypt for safety and was brought up at the Egyptian court. With Shishak's backing he now returned to Edom to rebel against Solomon.

SOLOMON'S JERUSALEM

Tyropoeon Valley

Solomon's city walls

Temple

Palace

Solomon's addition

The Jebusite and David's city

En-gihon

Pool of Siloam

In addition Shishak encouraged a young and able Israelite, Jeroboam. Jeroboam was one of Solomon's officials: he was so efficient in organizing the repair of the fortification of Jerusalem that Solomon made him responsible for the forced labour supplied by the tribes of Ephraim and Manasseh. But the prophetic party, which was opposed to Solomon's policy, saw in Jeroboam a man to whom the tribes of Israel might give their loyalty. The suggestion was made to Jeroboam (if he had not already thought of it) by the prophet Ahijah, of Shiloh. Solomon got to know of this, and Jeroboam left for Egypt. Here Shishak protected him until the death of Solomon, when Jeroboam's return became possible.

41

THE DIVISION OF THE KINGDOM

(1 Kings 12–16; 2 Chronicles 10–16)

930–880 BC

Solomon's son and successor was Rehoboam. Had he listened to wise advice, he might have prevented his kingdom from falling apart. When he went to Shechem to be installed as king, the representatives of the tribes approached him and asked him to lighten the heavy load of taxation and forced labour which his father had made them carry. Some of his counsellors urged him to give them a sympathetic reply; if he had done so, they might have been content to be his subjects. But he listened to young and inexperienced courtiers of his own generation, who advised him not to show any weakness. He gave them an unpromising answer, and that was enough. All the tribes except Judah and Benjamin revolted from him and set up Jeroboam as their ruler. He reigned as king of Israel; Rehoboam and his successors reigned as kings of Judah. Judah was Rehoboam's own tribe, and as for Benjamin, his capital city Jerusalem lay within its territory; this made it impossible for Benjamin to join the revolt of the northern tribes.

Jeroboam realized that, if his subjects continued to go to Solomon's temple in Jerusalem for the great festivals of pilgrimage and worship, they might continue to feel some loyalty to the dynasty of David. So he made two temples in his own kingdom into centres of religious worship – one at Bethel, in the south, not far from the frontier with Rehoboam's kingdom, and the other at Dan, in the far north. Whereas the invisible presence of Yahweh in Solomon's temple was supported by golden cherubs, symbolical creatures representing the forces of nature, that presence was symbolised at Dan and Bethel by golden bull-calves. These were dangerously similar to objects of Canaanite worship, and brought down on Jeroboam the condemnation of the prophetic party. It was they who described this king as "Jeroboam the son of Nebat, who made Israel to sin".

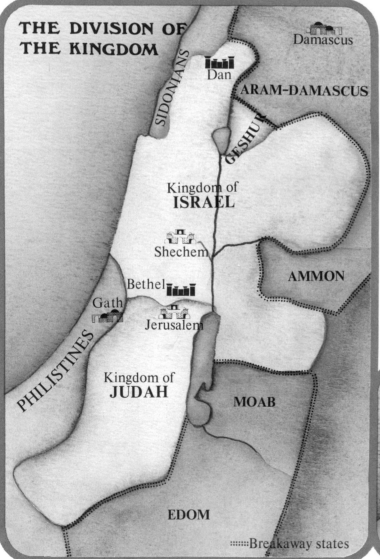

THE DIVISION OF THE KINGDOM

Damascus
Dan
SIDONIANS
ARAM-DAMASCUS
GESHUR
Kingdom of **ISRAEL**
Shechem
Bethel
Gath
Jerusalem
PHILISTINES
Kingdom of **JUDAH**
AMMON
MOAB
EDOM

......Breakaway states

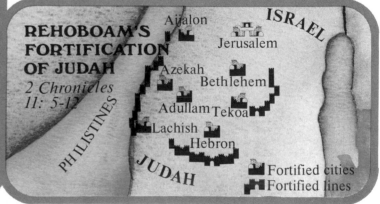

REHOBOAM'S FORTIFICATION OF JUDAH

2 Chronicles 11: 5-12

Aijalon
ISRAEL
Jerusalem
Azekah
Bethlehem
Adullam
Tekoa
Lachish
Hebron
PHILISTINES
JUDAH

Fortified cities
Fortified lines

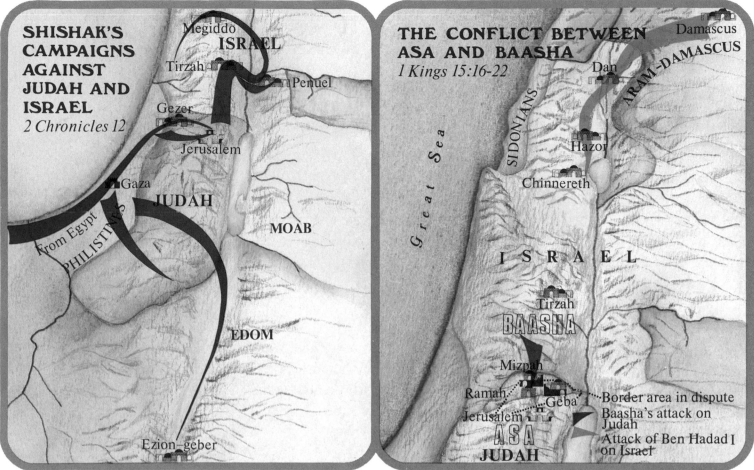

The kingdom of Judah remained with the dynasty of David for 350 years, descending from father to son through some sixteen generations. The pattern was quite different in the northern kingdom. Jeroboam's son Nadab was assassinated in a palace revolution, and the same process tended to repeat itself in every second generation. Only twice in the 210 years during which the northern kingdom lasted did a new dynasty succeed in establishing itself for more then two generations. The dynasty of Omri (founded about 881 BC) lasted through the reigns of four kings, and the dynasty of Jehu (founded about 841 BC) lasted through the reigns of five.

In the fifth year after the division of the kingdom, the land was invaded by Shishak, king of Egypt. The biblical account tells how he took away the ceremonial golden shields which adorned the temple in Jerusalem, and how Rehoboam had to replace them with bronze shields. Shishak's own account of the invasion is given in an inscription in the temple of Amun at Karnak in Egypt. He lists the cities in Asia which he conquered, and about 120 of them are recognizable as cities of Israel and Judah. Israel as well as Judah suffered at his hands; perhaps Jeroboam was not proving to be such an obedient subject king as Shishak had expected. At any rate the list of conquered cities includes Megiddo and other places in the Plain of Jezreel and across the Jordan.

The southern kingdom was gravely weakened by Shishak's invasion and was afraid that it might not stand up to an attack from the north. It therefore made an alliance with the Aramean kingdom of Damascus. This ensured that, if the kingdom of Israel took threatening action against Judah, the army of Damascus could threaten its frontier from the north-east. Such a situation arose during border wars between Asa of Judah and Baasha of Israel. About 885 BC Baasha penetrated as far into Judah as Ramah. Asa appealed for help to Ben-Hadad I of Damascus who seized the opportunity to invade Israel, driving Baasha back to his capital city at Tirzah. From then on the boundary ran between Mizpah and Geba.

THE RISE OF ASSYRIA AND FALL OF ISRAEL

(1 Kings 17–22; 2 Kings 1–17)

880–721 BC

Shortly before 880 BC an able army commander, Omri, seized power in the northern kingdom and established a dynasty which lasted for forty years.

Jeroboam's capital had been at Shechem but he or his successors moved it to Tirzah (Tell el-Far'a), about seven miles north-east of Shechem. Tirzah was the capital at the beginning of Omri's reign, but he chose a site seven miles north-west of Shechem to serve as a new capital, and built the city of Samaria there. Samaria's ability to resist long sieges was proved more than once in the next 160 years, and shows how wise Omri was in choosing it.

Omri conquered the kingdom of Moab, east of the Dead Sea, and also entered into a close economic alliance with the Phoenicians. This alliance was made firmer by a marriage between his son Ahab (who succeeded him in due course) and Jezebel, daughter of the Phoenician king. These moves helped him in the frequent frontier wars against the Arameans of Damascus, waged by himself and his successors. But the Phoenician alliance

BATTLES BETWEEN
ARAM AND ISRAEL
1 Kings 20,22

Hamath

Desert

PHOENICIA

ARAM-DAMASCUS

Damascus

Tyre

Great Sea

Aphek

ISRAEL

Samaria

Tirzah

Jerusalem

PHILISTINES

JUDAH

MOAB

had a harmful effect on the religious life of Israel: in particular, Jezebel encouraged the Canaanite worship of Baal and Asherah, which was very similar to the form of worship to which she was accustomed in her native land. This won for her and her husband the hostility of the prophets of Yahweh, chief of whom at this time was Elijah; in the long run their opposition played a large part in bringing down the dynasty.

The writer of 1 Kings tells of an occasion when there was peace for three years between Israel and Damascus, but he does not indicate the reason for this. The reason, however, is provided in the boastful records of the Assyrian king Shalmaneser III (859–823 BC). Shalmaneser led an army west from the Tigris, but found his way to the Mediterranean blocked at Qarqar, on the Syrian river Orontes, by an alliance of twelve kings. Two of these kings were the king of Damascus, Adadidri (called Ben-hadad in the Bible), who provided the largest infantry force (20,000 men), and Ahab of Israel, who provided the largest body of chariots (2,000 chariots), as well as 10,000 foot-soldiers. Shalmaneser claims a sweeping victory, describing the Orontes as dammed by the corpses of his foes; in fact, his opponents could claim some success, for he returned home and did not reappear in that part of the world for twelve years.

When he returned to the west, he found a new king on the throne of Israel – Jehu, who had just staged a revolt against the dynasty of Omri and wiped it out (841 BC). Jehu enjoyed the backing of the prophetic party, but his revolt weakened his country. This

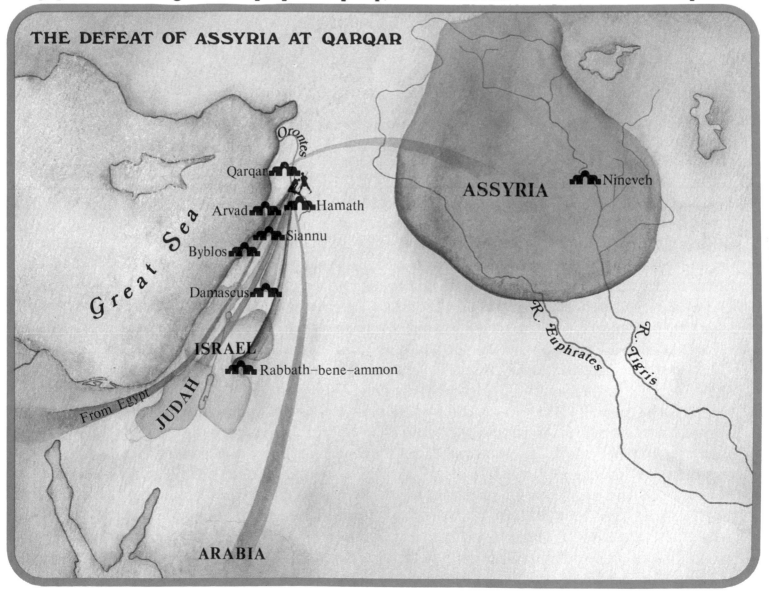

THE DEFEAT OF ASSYRIA AT QARQAR

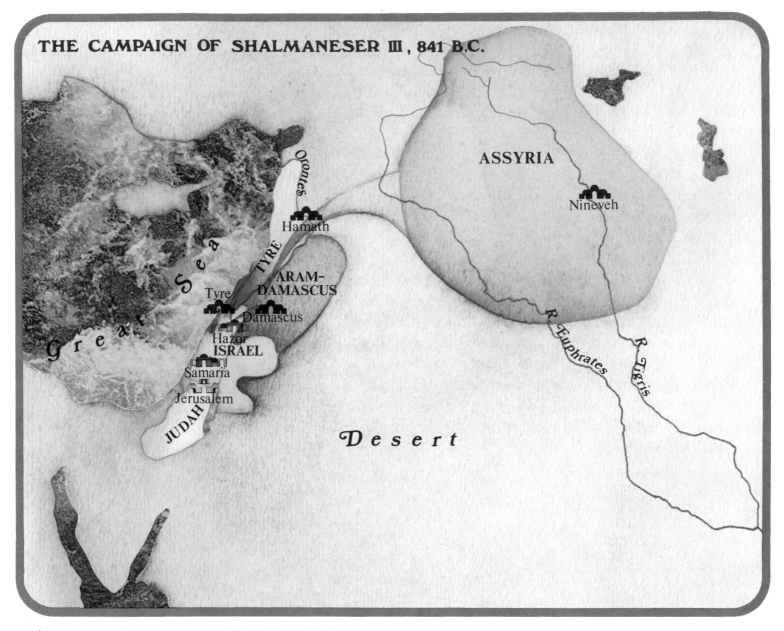

THE CAMPAIGN OF SHALMANESER III, 841 B.C.

time no resistance was offered to Shalmaneser: Jehu is listed as one of the rulers who paid homage to him and offered him tribute.

During the first forty years of the dynasty of Jehu, Israel's position became increasingly weaker in face of the rulers of Damascus. All her Transjordanian possessions were lost; in addition, the Arameans crossed the Jordan and moved down the Mediterranean coast as far as Gath, which they occupied. In 803 BC, however, an Assyrian king raided the kingdom of Damascus and made it a subject nation; Israel was able to breathe more freely and succeeded in regaining most of the land that had been lost.

The greatest king of the dynasty of Jehu was Jeroboam II (782-745 BC), under whom Israel became wealthier than it had been since Solomon's time. But as the rich grew more wealthy, the poorer members of society became worse off and weaker. In those days the prophets Amos and Hosea proclaimed that such an unjust society was doomed to collapse.

Nor was the situation much better in the southern kingdom, whose king Uzziah was contemporary with Jeroboam II. Uzziah made his kingdom stronger and wealthier but towards the end of his reign prophets arose with a message quite like that which other prophets had delivered farther north. Micah, from the Judean countryside, reminded the people of the ancient covenant by insisting that what Yahweh required of his people was "to do justice, and to love kindness, and to walk humbly with your God". Isaiah, who lived in Jerusalem, and was called to his prophetic ministry "in the year that king Uzziah died", continued to try to waken the national conscience for forty years. Long before those forty years came to an end, the northern kingdom of Israel had been wiped off the map.

The death of Jeroboam II was followed by trouble from inside and outside his kingdom. His successor, the last member of the dynasty of Jehu, reigned only six months; then he was assassinated and replaced by a usurper. About the same time a new king came to power in Assyria, Tiglath-pileser III. Tiglath-pileser not only raided his western neighbours and imposed tribute on them, as some of his predecessors had done: he aimed at building up an empire. Menahem, king of Israel, saw the wisdom of giving in to Tiglath-pileser's demands: he kept his throne by paying the Assyrian king an

DAMASCUS CONQUERS TRANSJORDAN
2 Kings 10:32,33;12,17,18.

Damascus

SIDONIANS

Great Sea

Hazor

Ashtaroth

Lost to Damascus

ISRAEL

R. Jordan

AMMON

Gath

PHILISTINES

Aroer

JUDAH

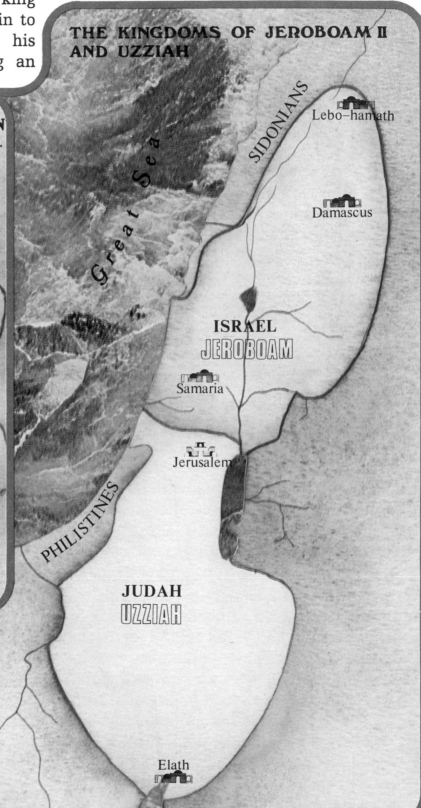

THE KINGDOMS OF JEROBOAM II AND UZZIAH

Lebo–hamath

SIDONIANS

Great Sea

Damascus

ISRAEL
JEROBOAM

Samaria

Jerusalem

PHILISTINES

JUDAH
UZZIAH

Elath

enormous tribute, which he raised by taxing all the wealthy citizens of his kingdom.

There was, however, an anti-Assyrian group in Israel, which found a leader in Pekah, an army commander in Transjordan. Pekah rebelled against Menahem's son and successor, assassinated him, and reigned in his place. He then formed an anti-Assyrian alliance with Rezin, king of Damascus. Rezin and Pekah tried to bring Judah into their alliance by deposing Ahaz, Uzziah's grandson, and appointing their own king of Judah in his place. Ahaz took fright and sent an urgent message for help to Tiglath-pileser. This was the occasion of some of Isaiah's greatest prophecies: he warned Ahaz against the folly of his action, assuring him that Rezin and Pekah could not last long, and that he should put his trust in God, not in Tiglath-pileser. But Ahaz thought he knew better. Tiglath-pileser marched west in 732 BC overrunning Gilead and the country as far south as Megiddo. He dealt with Rezin and Pekah as he would have done in any case. Rezin's kingdom was made an Assyrian province; so was the northern part of the kingdom of Israel. Pekah's subjects rose against him and put Hoshea on the throne in his place. Hoshea in haste did homage to the Assyrian king, and was allowed to keep the territory between the Plain of Jezreel and the frontier of Judah.

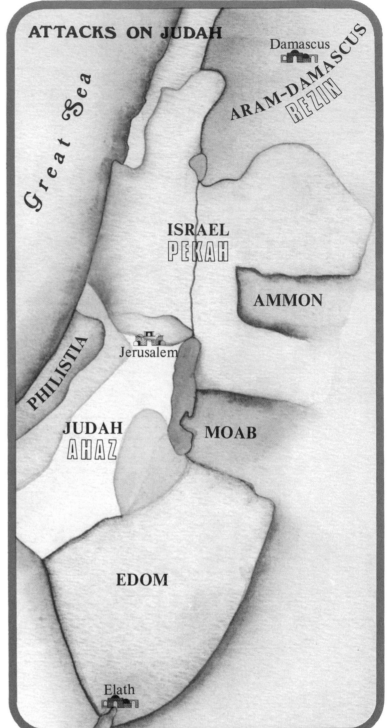

But Ahaz too had to pay homage to the Assyrian king and undertake to pay tribute to him year by year. It was over a century before the kingdom of Judah got rid of the Assyrian yoke. "Ahaz by his unbelief had not only *disestablished* himself; he had mortgaged the hope of Israel" (G. A. Smith). As for Hoshea, he was later persuaded by false promises of Egyptian help to rebel against Assyria.

Shalmaneser V, who was now king of Assyria, marched west and took Hoshea captive. The city of Samaria stood out against the Assyrian siege-engines for three years, but it fell in 721 BC, just after Shalmaneser V had been succeeded on the Assyrian throne by Sargon II. Hoshea's kingdom became the Assyrian province of Samaria. Many of its inhabitants were deported to other parts of the Assyrian Empire (as the inhabitants of Galilee had been deported eleven years before), and were replaced by settlers from elsewhere. These settlers intermarried with the Israelites who were left in the land. This was the origin of the Samaritan nation, which survives as a tiny remnant to the present day.

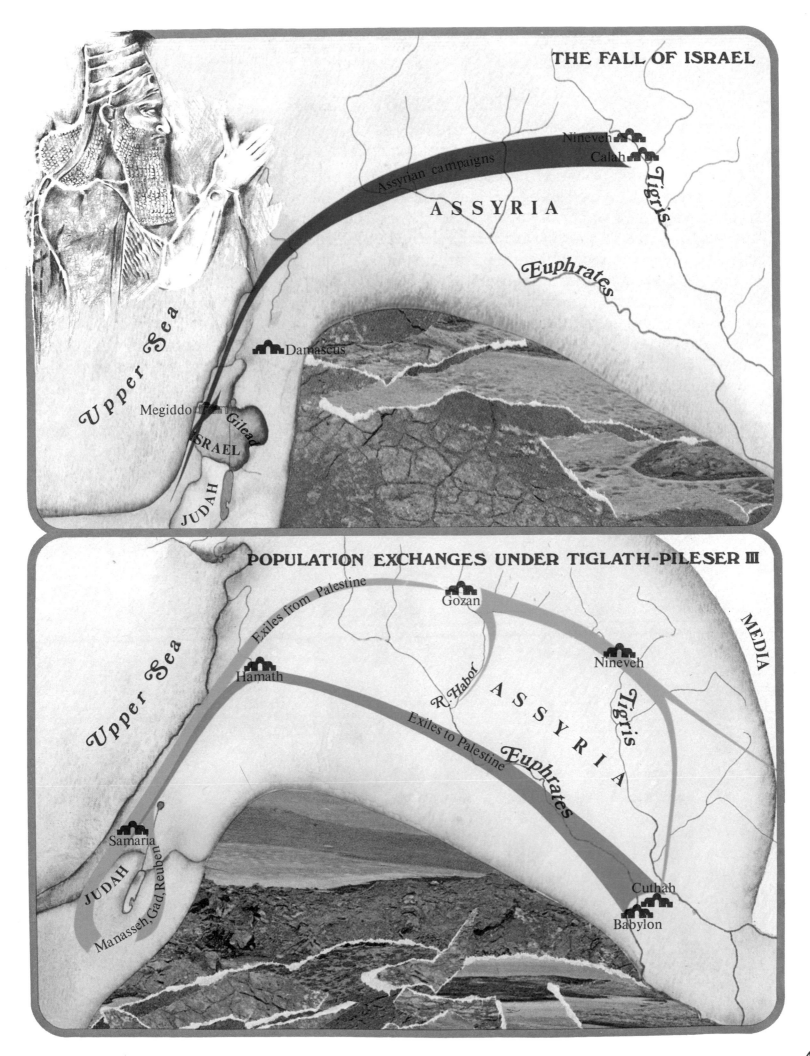

THE FALL OF ISRAEL

Assyrian campaigns

ASSYRIA

Nineveh
Calah

Tigris

Euphrates

Upper Sea

Damascus

Megiddo Gilead

ISRAEL

JUDAH

POPULATION EXCHANGES UNDER TIGLATH-PILESER III

Exiles from Palestine

Gozan

MEDIA

Nineveh

Hamath

R. Habor

Exiles to Palestine

Tigris

ASSYRIA

Euphrates

Upper Sea

Samaria

JUDAH

Manasseh, Gad, Reuben

Cuthah

Babylon

THE FALL OF JUDAH

(2 Kings 22–25)

721–587 BC

After the fall of Israel, Judah remained as a self-governing monarchy within the Assyrian Empire. The Assyrians believed that their gods had enabled them to gain military and imperial power, and they expected subject-nations within their empire to recognize this in some practical way. During the reign of Ahaz, for example, various objects of Assyrian worship were introduced into the Jerusalem temple, alongside the altar of that God who had forbidden his people to have any other gods in his presence.

In 705 BC Sargon of Assyria died and was succeeded by his son Sennacherib. Hezekiah, son of Ahaz, and some of his neighbours were encouraged by Egypt and Babylon to rebel against Assyria. Isaiah warned Hezekiah of the danger of this policy, but his warning went unheeded until the danger became too plain to be ignored. When he declared his independence of Assyria, Hezekiah cleared the Assyrian sacred objects out of the temple, and this is recorded with approval by the Hebrew historians.

But Sennacherib methodically put down one revolt after another throughout his territory. Having dealt with Babylon, he marched to Phoenicia, and from there moved south along the coastal road, punishing the cities which had rebelled. Then he turned inland to deal with Judah (701 BC). His records claim that he took forty-six fortified cities of Judah. One was Lachish: a bas-relief showing its siege and capture adorned Sennacherib's palace

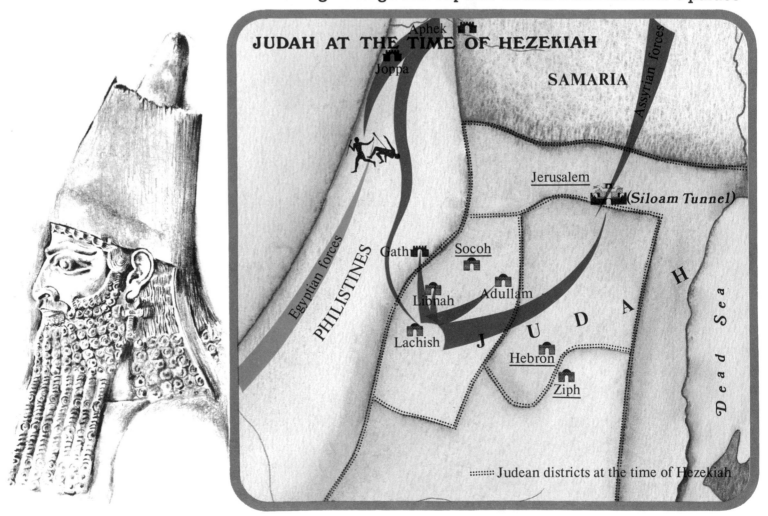

JUDAH AT THE TIME OF HEZEKIAH

Aphek
Joppa
SAMARIA
Assyrian forces
Jerusalem
(Siloam Tunnel)
Egyptian forces
PHILISTINES
Gath
Socoh
Libnah
Adullam
Lachish
J U D A H
Hebron
Ziph
Dead Sea

:::::: Judean districts at the time of Hezekiah

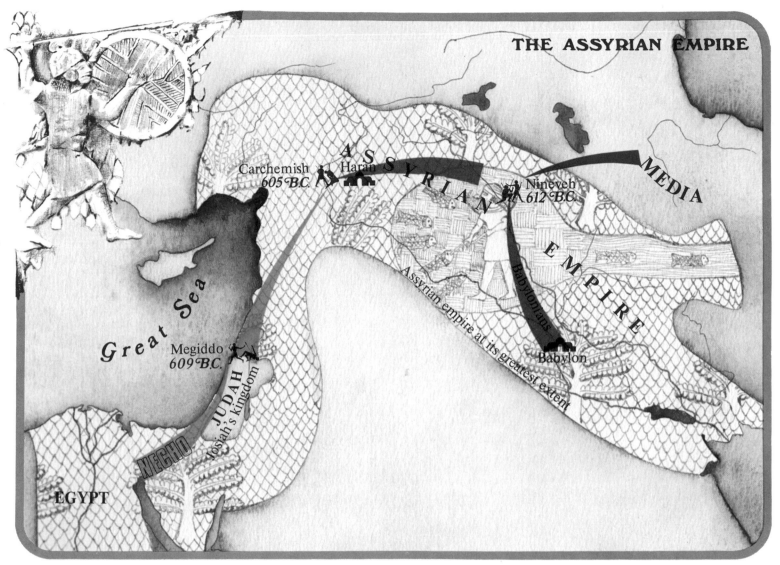

MEDIA

Carchemish
605 B.C.

Haran

A S S Y R I A N

E M P I R E

Nineveh
612 B.C.

Babylonians

Assyrian empire at its greatest extent

Babylon

Great Sea

Megiddo
609 B.C.

JUDAH
Josiah's kingdom

NECHO

EGYPT

at Nineveh; it is now in the British Museum, London. From Lachish he sent a military force to Jerusalem, 30 miles to the north-east, threatening to treat it as he had treated the other Judean cities. Although Hezekiah sent him an apology, promising to pay whatever tribute Sennacherib might demand, Sennacherib decided to take Jerusalem and abolish the Judean monarchy. However, news of an Egyptian force marching against him drew him away and Jerusalem was spared. But Judah remained subject to Assyria for the rest of the reign of Hezekiah and during the reigns of his son Manasseh and his grandson Amon.

Preparing Jerusalem to face an Assyrian siege, Hezekiah improved its water-supply by having a tunnel dug through the rock from the Virgin's Fountain (Gihon) in the Kidron valley so that water was carried from there into the pool of Siloam south of the city. Water flows through this tunnel to the present day.

Manasseh was a loyal subject of the Assyrians and, like his grandfather Ahaz, placed objects of Assyrian worship in the temple. On one occasion an Assyrian king suspected him of disloyalty and took him captive to Babylon, but evidently the suspicion proved to be unfounded and Manasseh was restored to his throne. During his reign the Assyrian Empire reached its greatest extent, especially under Sennacherib's grandson Ashurbanipal (669–626 BC). But after his death his great empire collapsed, and in 612 BC Nineveh, its capital city, fell before a combined attack by the Medes from the east and the Babylonians from the south.

With Ashurbanipal's death the Assyrian grip on Judah was loosened. Josiah, the young king of Judah (639–609 BC), once more expelled all trace of Assyrian worship from the temple and started a nation-wide reform of religious practice. Indeed, he was able to carry

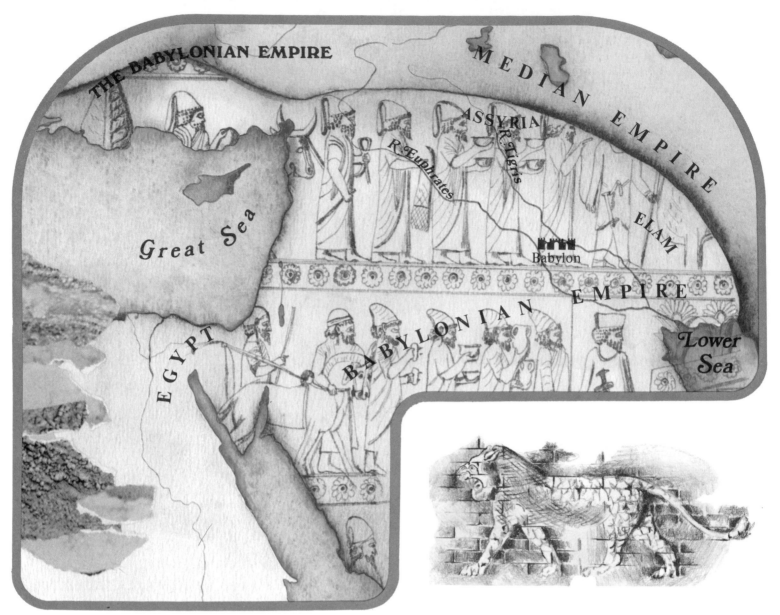

out this policy in what had been the northern kingdom as well as in Judah: the Assyrians could no longer prevent him. His policy was in line with the law-code in the book of Deuteronomy, a copy of which had been discovered in the temple while it was being repaired. Among other things, Josiah closed down all the sanctuaries in the country except the temple in Jerusalem, so that everyone had to worship there.

The king of Egypt, Necho II, hoped to preserve something of the weakened Assyrian Empire to balance the rising power of Media and Babylonia. As he marched along the Palestinian coastal road, making for Carchemish on the Euphrates, where the river could be forded, Josiah tried to check his advance in the pass of Megiddo, but was killed. For three or four years Necho dominated all the lands west of the Euphrates, but in 605 BC he was thoroughly defeated at Carchemish by the army of Nebuchadrezzar of Babylon, and had to retreat to Egypt.

Now the whole territory between the Euphrates and the Egyptian border fell under the rule of Nebuchadrezzar, who established a Babylonian Empire. Josiah's son Jehoiakim, forced to pay tribute, was encouraged by Egypt to revolt. The revolt was put down by Nebuchadrezzar in 597 BC, and Judah was given one further chance. Nebuchadrezzar placed another son of Josiah, Zedekiah, on the throne in Jerusalem. When, in spite of the warnings of the prophet Jeremiah, Zedekiah rebelled, Nebuchadrezzar took a fearful vengeance. Jerusalem was taken after a siege of eighteen months, the temple and other great buildings were destroyed, many of the leading men were executed, and Zedekiah

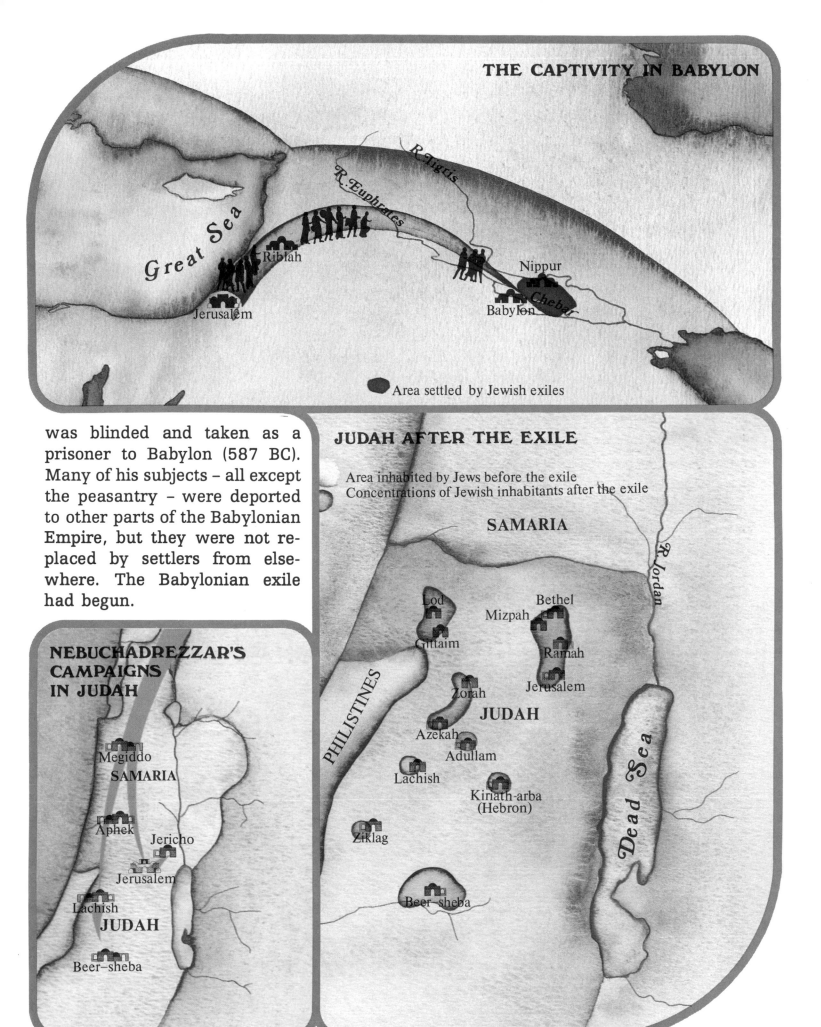

Area settled by Jewish exiles

was blinded and taken as a prisoner to Babylon (587 BC). Many of his subjects – all except the peasantry – were deported to other parts of the Babylonian Empire, but they were not replaced by settlers from elsewhere. The Babylonian exile had begun.

JUDAH AFTER THE EXILE

Area inhabited by Jews before the exile
Concentrations of Jewish inhabitants after the exile

SAMARIA

R. Jordan

Lod

Bethel

Mizpah

Gittaim

Ramah

Zorah

Jerusalem

JUDAH

PHILISTINES

Azekah

Adullam

Lachish

Kiriath-arba
(Hebron)

Ziklag

Dead Sea

Beer-sheba

NEBUCHADREZZAR'S CAMPAIGNS IN JUDAH

Megiddo

SAMARIA

Aphek

Jericho

Jerusalem

Lachish

JUDAH

Beer-sheba

EXILE AND RETURN

(Ezra 1–10; Nehemiah 1–13; Daniel; Esther)

587–332 BC

Jeremiah and Ezekiel agreed that hope for the nation's future lay with the people who had been deported. Although the exiles did preserve the knowledge of God, they were unable to return home and plant the knowledge of God there. In the events that made it possible for them to do so nearly fifty years after the downfall of the monarchy, they were taught to recognize the hand of God, over-ruling events in other nations in order to help his people Israel.

In 550 BC the Median empire, which stretched from modern Iran westwards into Asia Minor, was defeated by Cyrus of Persia. Under the leadership of Cyrus the new Medo-Persian Empire quickly conquered several neighbouring territories. In 539 BC Cyrus entered Babylon and had himself installed as king there. One of the first things he did after occupying Babylon was to make a law allowing the Jewish exiles to return home and live there under a governor who was answerable to him. About the same time he granted permission for the temple in Jerusalem to be rebuilt and for the sacrificial services there to start again.

These actions helped Cyrus politically. He gained good will in a similar way in other parts of his empire. But the Jewish prophets saw him as the instrument of the God of Israel.

The Jews who returned found the prospect of re-establishing themselves in their abandoned homeland a depressing one. Those who had stayed in Judah did not welcome them. They restored the great altar in the temple court and may even have made a start on the temple itself, but there were too many discouragements for them to carry the work through. Their Samaritan neighbours offered to help them rebuild the temple, but their offer was refused. The rejected Samaritans then put various obstacles in their way.

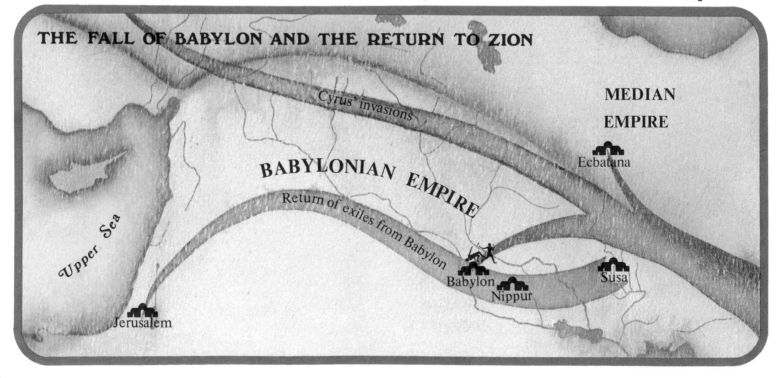

THE FALL OF BABYLON AND THE RETURN TO ZION

Cyrus' invasions

MEDIAN EMPIRE

Ecbatana

BABYLONIAN EMPIRE

Return of exiles from Babylon

Upper Sea

Babylon

Nippur

Susa

Jerusalem

However, in 520 BC fresh encouragement was given to them by their governor Zerubbabel (a descendant of the royal family of Judah), by the high priest Jeshua and by the prophets Haggai and Zechariah. An order was obtained from the new Persian king, Darius, confirming the permission previously given by Cyrus. A new temple was dedicated seventy years after the previous one had been burnt by the Babylonians. From this time until AD 70 we have to do with the period of the Second Temple.

One thing the Persian kings had not allowed: that was the rebuilding of the walls around Jerusalem, so as to make it a fortified city. A fortified city could become a base for revolt. At least one attempt was made to build the city walls, but a message came promptly from the Persian court ordering the builders to stop.

Later there was a change in royal policy. The Jews proved loyal to the Persian Empire and in an area where revolt might break out at any time it could be to the advantage of the Persian king to have one fortified city whose loyalty could be depended on. Whatever his motives, in 445 BC Artaxerxes I of Persia gave powers to a Jew named Nehemiah, who had been his chief cup-bearer, to leave the Persian court at Susa and go to Judah as governor and rebuild the walls of Jerusalem. Nehemiah's adventures while the walls were being built are described in his diaries, which are included in the Bible book bearing his name.

About the same time Artaxerxes permitted another Jew, a priest and legal expert named Ezra, to draw up a new constitution for the province of Judah on the basis of the law of Israel's God

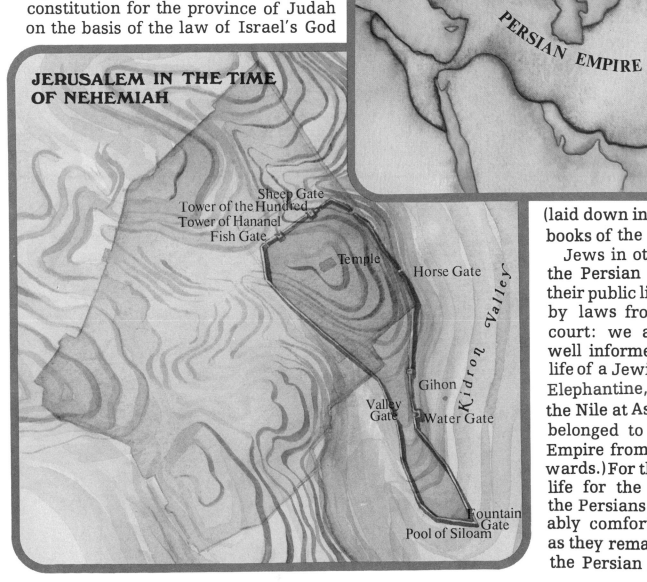

JERUSALEM IN THE TIME OF NEHEMIAH

Sheep Gate
Tower of the Hundred
Tower of Hananel
Fish Gate
Temple
Horse Gate
Kidron Valley
Gihon
Valley Gate
Water Gate
Fountain Gate
Pool of Siloam

THE PERSIAN EMPIRE 6th to 4th cent. B.C.

PERSIAN EMPIRE

(laid down in the first five books of the Bible).

Jews in other parts of the Persian Empire had their public life regulated by laws from the royal court: we are specially well informed about the life of a Jewish colony on Elephantine, an island in the Nile at Aswan. (Egypt belonged to the Persian Empire from 525 BC onwards.) For the most part, life for the Jews under the Persians was reasonably comfortable, so long as they remained loyal to the Persian government.

THE RULE OF GREECE

(Daniel 11:3–30; 1 Maccabees 1)

332–167 BC

The Persian Empire had lasted for just over 200 years when it was overthrown by a mightier power from the west. By military conquest and diplomatic skill Philip II, king of Macedonia, united the whole of Greece under his rule. He planned to lead a united army of Macedonians and Greeks against the Persians, but was assassinated in 336 BC before he could make a beginning. His plan, with his kingship, was inherited by his twenty-year-old son Alexander.

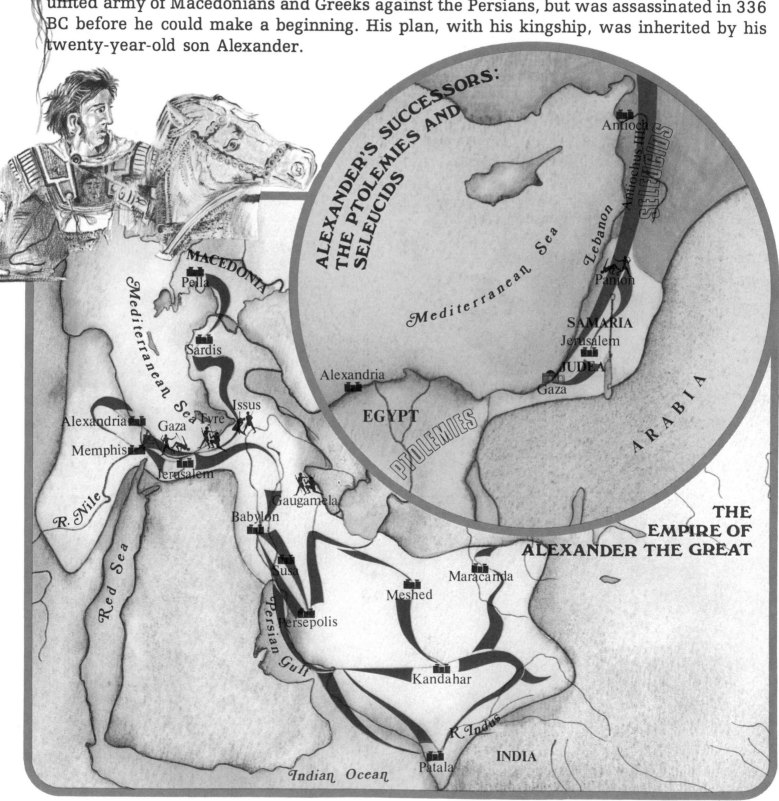

ALEXANDER'S SUCCESSORS:
THE PTOLEMIES AND
SELEUCIDS

THE
EMPIRE OF
ALEXANDER THE GREAT

In 334 BC Alexander led his army into Asia. He soon conquered Asia Minor, and a victory at Issus, on the Gulf of Alexandretta (333 BC), opened his way south into Syria. His progress was held up by the resistance of Tyre, which was taken in July, 332 BC, after a siege of seven months. As he marched south, Samaria and Judea submitted to him. Gaza, like Tyre, offered resistance but was taken after a siege, and Alexander marched into Egypt and added that country to his empire. There, in 331 BC, he founded the city which bears his name to this day – Alexandria.

Then he returned through Syria, crossed the Euphrates and Tigris, and inflicted his final defeat on the Persians at Gaugamela, east of the Tigris (October, 331 BC). The Persian Empire was now Alexander's. He continued his eastward advance as far as the Indus, adding to his empire the countries now known as Afghanistan and Pakistan. He might have gone still farther, but his followers decided that they had come far enough and won sufficient glory. On his way back Alexander died of a fever at Babylon.

His empire was soon split up after his death. His leading generals fought one another to become emperor, and the empire was divided among them. Two of its divisions are important for us: Egypt, which was ruled from Alexandria by Ptolemy I and his successors, and Syria and the lands farther east, ruled from Antioch on the Orontes by Seleucus I and his successors. We call those two dynasties the Ptolemaic and the Seleucid.

Until about 200 BC the rule of the Ptolemaic dynasty extended from Egypt into Asia as far north as Lebanon; it thus included the Holy Land. Life for the people of Judea was quiet and well-ordered: they had a Ptolemaic governor instead of a Persian one, and paid their taxes to Alexandria instead of to the Persian court. The tax-system was very efficiently organized. Many Jews found their way to Alexandria and settled there. Before long one of the five districts into which Alexandria was divided was totally Jewish.

The Jews of Alexandria soon learned to speak Greek (for Alexandria was a Greek-speaking city and remained so for 1,000 years). In a generation or two they forgot the language they had spoken in the Holy Land. They were thus no longer able to understand the sacred scriptures, which were written in Hebrew. Accordingly, the scriptures were translated from Hebrew into Greek, so that they could be read in the synagogues of Alexandria in a language which the congregation understood. To begin with, it was the first five books of the Bible that were translated. This is the translation that is commonly known as the Septuagint. The Septuagint translation of the Old Testament became important later because it was used by Paul and other Christian missionaries when they took the Christian message to the Greek-speaking lands of the eastern Mediterranean world.

About 200 BC a king of the Seleucid dynasty in Syria, Antiochus III, gave battle to the Ptolemaic forces. He defeated them at a place called Panion, near the source of the Jordan (the place referred to in the New Testament as Caesarea Philippi). The result was that the Ptolemaic forces were driven out of Asia, and the land between Lebanon and the Egyptian border now belonged to the empire of the Seleucids.

At first this made little difference to the Jews of Judea, except that their taxes had now to be paid to Antioch and not to Alexandria. Antiochus III ruled the whole of Asia Minor, and he encouraged Jews to settle in various parts of that peninsula. But his ambitions brought him into conflict with the Romans, who by this time had taken Greece under their protection. A Roman army defeated him in Asia Minor, in 190 BC. He was forced to give up many of his possessions in Asia Minor and also to pay a heavy fine to the victors. To raise the money he had to increase the taxes paid by his subjects. The people of Judea began to feel that they had been better off under the Ptolemies. Moreover, the need to raise money quickly was so great that Antiochus and his successors did not hesitate to raid temples, in which wealthy people used to deposit their treasures for protection by the gods. The temple in Jerusalem did not escape one or two raids of this kind.

In 175 BC Antiochus III's younger son, Antiochus IV, ascended the Seleucid throne. He had been educated in Rome, and had no wish to challenge the power of the Romans. But he thought he saw an opportunity of restoring his power and his possessions by extending his rule over Egypt. In 169 BC he entered Egypt and was accepted as regent on behalf of the boy king, who was his nephew. But there was a party in Egypt opposed to him, and it organized a revolt against him. Next year he invaded Egypt in order to put down the revolt. No one could successfully resist him, and he was well on his way to Alexandria when his ambition was frustrated.

Antiochus thought that the Romans were sufficiently busy with a war against the Macedonians for him to take over Egypt without their interference. But the Romans ended their war with the Macedonians quickly and successfully, and sent a detachment of warships to the harbour of Alexandria. A small body of Roman officials and troops was put ashore and set out to meet Antiochus as he approached the city. When they met, the Roman leader ordered him sternly to get out of Egypt. Antiochus had no choice but to obey.

News of this had gone before him to Judea: it was rumoured, in fact, that he had been killed. The people rose and threw out a man whom Antiochus had recently appointed high priest in Jerusalem. When Antiochus arrived in Judea from Egypt, he treated Jerusalem as a rebellious city and placed it under martial law.

Now that Antiochus had been thrown out of Egypt, Judea lay on the south-western frontier of his kingdom. That frontier required to be protected, and it could not be adequately protected under rulers on whose loyalty Antiochus felt he could not rely. Therefore he destroyed the system of government which Judea and Jerusalem had enjoyed since the return from the Babylonian exile. Under that system, the high priest and other temple rulers governed the Jewish people. Now Jerusalem was governed like a Greek city, and only those who were prepared to support the king's policy could be enrolled as citizens.

Worse than that was to follow. The king's advisers assured him that it was the Jews' religion that made it impossible for them to be properly absorbed into his kingdom; they therefore urged him to abolish their religion. This he attempted to do. All the special practices of the Jewish religion were forbidden, copies of the sacred scriptures were destroyed, and at the end of 167 BC the worship of Israel's God in the temple of Jerusalem was discontinued. In his place a pagan deity was installed – called by the Syrians the Lord of Heaven and by the Greeks Olympian Zeus. (Antiochus claimed to represent the presence or manifestation of this god upon earth; that is the meaning of the title Epiphanes, "manifest", commonly added to his name).

On top of the great altar of burnt offering in the temple court a smaller altar was erected, and on this smaller altar sacrifices were offered to the usurping god. The Jews called this altar "the abomination of desolation" – a phrase which in their own language was a mocking distortion of the title "the Lord of Heaven". Many Jews refused to accept this interference with their age-old worship, and were prepared to die rather than be untrue to the living God.

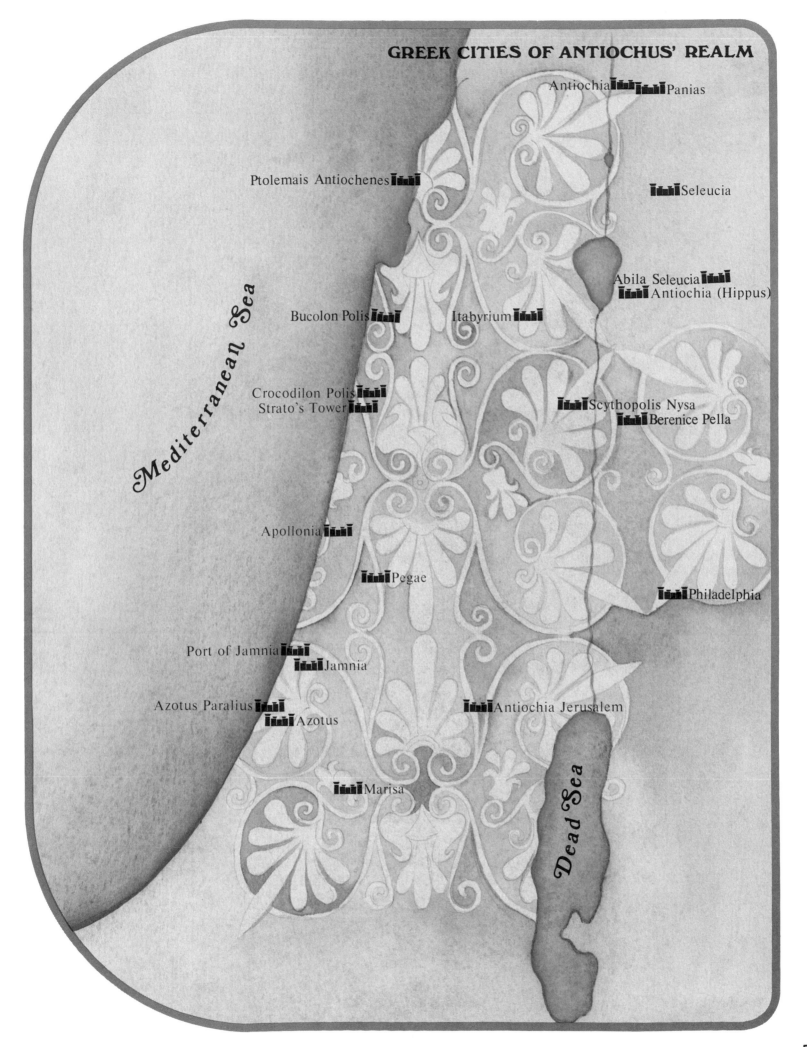

GREEK CITIES OF ANTIOCHUS' REALM

Antiochia Panias

Ptolemais Antiochenes

Seleucia

Abila Seleucia
Antiochia (Hippus)

Bucolon Polis   Itabyrium

Crocodilon Polis   Scythopolis Nysa
Strato's Tower   Berenice Pella

Mediterranean Sea

Apollonia

Pegae

Philadelphia

Port of Jamnia
Jamnia

Azotus Paralius   Antiochia Jerusalem
Azotus

Marisa

Dead Sea

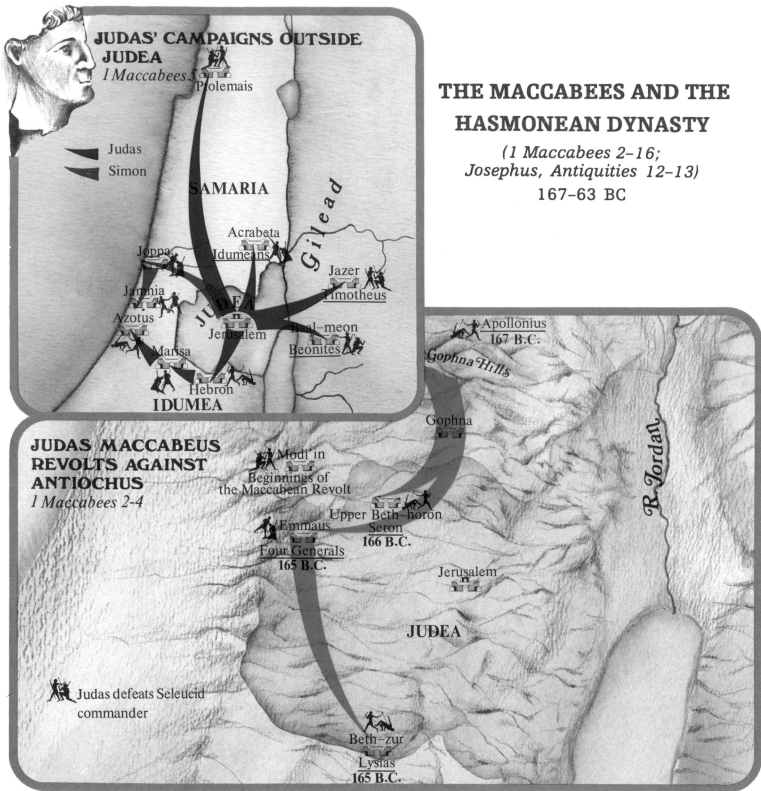

JUDAS' CAMPAIGNS OUTSIDE JUDEA
1 Maccabees 5

Ptolemais

Judas
Simon

SAMARIA

Gilead

Acrabeta

Joppa
Idumeans

Jazer
Timotheus

Jamnia
Azotus

JUDEA

Jerusalem

Baal-meon

Marisa

Beonites

Hebron

IDUMEA

THE MACCABEES AND THE HASMONEAN DYNASTY
*(1 Maccabees 2–16;
Josephus, Antiquities 12–13)*
167–63 BC

Apollonius
167 B.C.

Gophna Hills

Gophna

JUDAS MACCABEUS REVOLTS AGAINST ANTIOCHUS
1 Maccabees 2–4

Modi'in
Beginnings of
the Maccabean Revolt

Upper Beth-horon
Seron
166 B.C.

Emmaus
Four Generals
165 B.C.

Jerusalem

R. Jordan

JUDEA

Judas defeats Seleucid
commander

Beth-zur
Lysias
165 B.C.

There were two bodies of people in Judea who were resolutely opposed to the king's policy. One was called the Hasideans, people who kept to the pure Jewish religion and refused to admit any pagan tendencies. Many of them now died as martyrs for their faith. The other group consisted of those who took up arms to resist any interference with their national worship and way of life. They found a leader in an elderly priest named Mattathias. When an officer of the king came to Modi'in, Mattathias's home town, in Western Judea, and ordered the leading men to sacrifice on a pagan altar which had been set up so that they might show their loyalty by this means, Mattathias not only refused an invitation to offer a sacrifice, but killed the first man who ran up to the altar to show his loyalty by offering one, and then for good measure killed the king's officer also. Thus the standard of revolt was raised. Mattathias called on all those who had a zeal for God to come and join him; then he and his sons, with their followers, took to the Gophna hills to launch a campaign of guerrilla warfare.

Mattathias did not live long after this, but his five sons showed themselves able leaders of the Jewish rebels. One of the five, Judas, was remarkably skilled as a guerrilla leader. He came to be known as Judas Maccabeus, Judas the hammer (or hammerer). In Samaria, in the highlands of Beth-horon, at Emmaus and Beth-zur, he and his followers defeated a succession of well-equipped armies sent against them by Antiochus. The Hasideans recognized in him a man who had been raised up by God for the defence of true religion, and they gave him their support.

Before long Antiochus realized that his advisers had sadly misled him when they assured him that the abolition of the Jewish religion would solve all his problems in Judea. He was anxious to engage in military action beyond the Euphrates, where the rising power of Parthia threatened to reduce his own power, and he could not afford to have a large military force compelled to remain in Judea. Accordingly a truce was arranged; the ban on the Jewish religion was cancelled. Judas and his followers took advantage of the truce to occupy the temple area. The pagan altar was demolished and all the other evidences of the cult of Olympian Zeus were removed. The temple was purified and in December, 164 BC, it was solemnly rededicated to the worship of the God of Israel. The anniversary of this event has been celebrated by Jews ever since then as the Feast of Dedication (Hanukkah).

Now that the Jewish religion might be practised freely once again, the Hasideans were disposed to be content: this was what they had fought for. But Judas and his brothers, with their followers, had other ideas. Judas and his family are best known as the Hasmoneans, after one of their ancestors called Hasmon; to call them Maccabees is not strictly accurate, since Maccabeus was a name specially given to Judas. The Hasmoneans reckoned that, since they had won religious freedom by armed resistance, they might go on to win political independence in the same way. This meant further fighting outside Judea in the course of which Judas was killed (160 BC). He was succeeded as leader by his brother Jonathan.

After the death of Antiochus IV (164 BC) there was a long period of rivalry for the

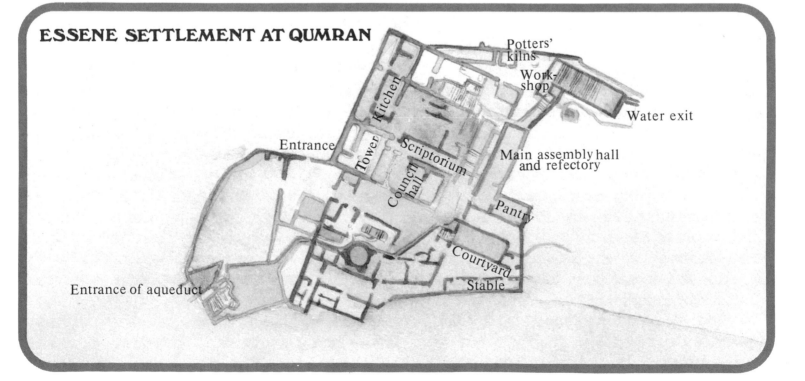

ESSENE SETTLEMENT AT QUMRAN

Potters' kilns
Work-shop
Water exit
Kitchen
Entrance
Tower
Scriptorium
Council hall
Main assembly hall and refectory
Pantry
Courtyard
Stable
Entrance of aqueduct

succession to the Seleucid throne, bran between two-ches of the royal family. The Hasmoneans were helped by this division in the enemy ranks, especially when one side or the other, recognizing what a fine body of fighting men the Hasmone-ans commanded, tried to enlist them as allies. In 153 BC one of the claimants to the Seleucid kingship, Alexander Balas (who gave himself out to be a son of Antiochus IV), offered to make Jonathan high priest of Israel if he would support him. Jonathan accepted the offer.

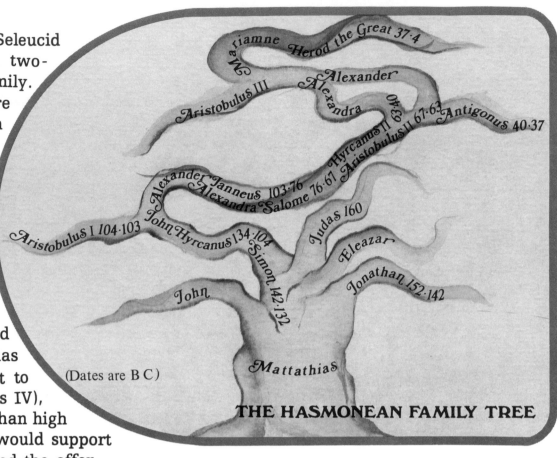

(Dates are B C)

THE HASMONEAN FAMILY TREE

From the time of Solomon the high priesthood in the Jerusalem temple descended from father to son in the family of Zadok (the priest who anointed Solomon king). Antiochus IV had taken the high priesthood away from the family of Zadok, but many pious Jews believed that no one could be approved by God as high priest except a member of that family. The Hasmoneans were priests, to be sure, but were not descendants of Zadok. The Hasideans disapproved of Jonathan's acceptance of the sacred office, and this in due course led to the end of their alliance with the Hasmoneans. Another group of pious Jews so thoroughly disagreed with Jonathan's action that they withdrew to the wilderness and set themselves up as a new miniature Israel, the righteous remnant of the faithless nation, north-west of the Dead Sea, at the place now called Qumran. It is to this community that we owe the Dead Sea Scrolls, a library belonging to the period 130 BC–AD 70.

Under Jonathan's brother Simon, who succeeded him in the leadership and high priesthood, national independence was gained in 141 BC. At a national assembly held in the following year, Simon was formally proclaimed governor of the nation, commander-in-chief of the army, and hereditary high priest. The threefold authority was handed down to his son and grandsons after him.

From national independence the Hasmonean dynasty proceeded to national expansion. Simon's son John Hyrcanus (134–104 BC) and his grandsons Aristobulus I (104–103 BC) and Alexander Janneus (103–76 BC) extended the borders of their realm until it included the whole of Palestine and a good part of Transjordan. Aristobulus took the title king and wore a royal crown. He and his brother Alexander Janneus were more like Greek rulers, seeking to become politically powerful and to gain military success, with little thought for culture or religion.

Under Alexander Janneus the breach between the Hasideans (now represented by the party of the Pharisees) and the Hasmonean family became complete. The Pharisees were suspected by Alexander of helping a rebellion which it took him six years to put down.

When he put it down (88 BC) he had 800 captives publicly crucified, including a number of leading Pharisees.

A welcome relief for the Pharisees was introduced when Alexander died and his widow, Salome Alexandra, reigned in his place. She favoured the Pharisees and raised them to positions of influence in the national council (the Sanhedrin). The party in the council on which earlier rulers had relied was the party of the Sadducees, drawn mainly from upper-class land owners.

Alexandra, as a woman, could be neither high priest nor commander of the army. Her elder son, Hyrcanus II, became high priest; her younger son, Aristobulus II, was appointed army commander. Aristobulus was an ambitious prince; his elder brother was quite unambitious but was so weak-minded that he was easily used by more ambitious politicians. Among these was a man of Edomite descent named Antipater. The Edomites (or Idumeans) had been conquered by John Hyrcanus I and forced to accept the Jewish religion.

When Alexandra died in 67 BC, a dispute over the succession broke out between Aristobulus and the supporters of Hyrcanus. It was the worst possible time for such a dispute, because it gave an excuse for intervention to the Roman general Pompey. Pompey was sent to the Near East in 66 BC to settle affairs in that part of the world in the interests of Rome. In 64 BC he was in Syria, reorganising that territory as a Roman province. He was invited to settle the dispute in Judea and readily accepted

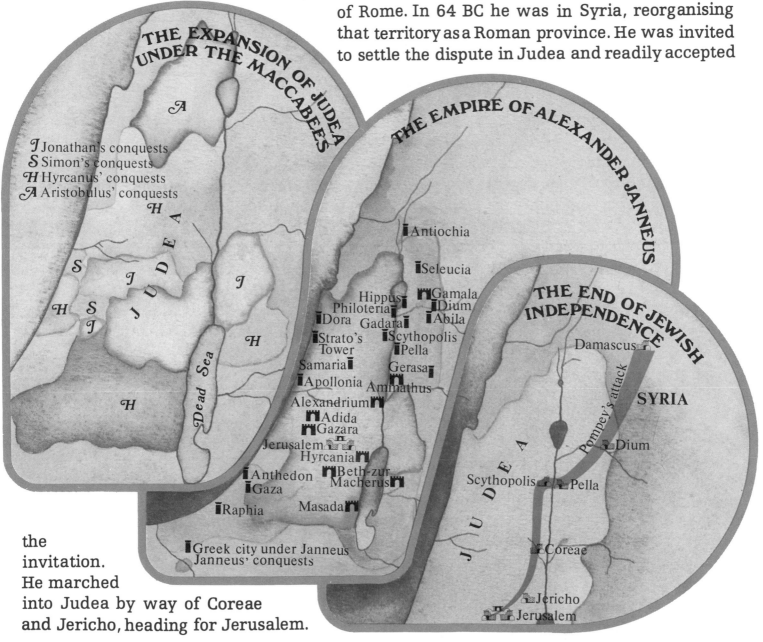

THE EXPANSION OF JUDEA UNDER THE MACCABEES

𝒥 Jonathan's conquests
𝒮 Simon's conquests
ℋ Hyrcanus' conquests
𝒜 Aristobulus' conquests

JUDEA
Dead Sea

THE EMPIRE OF ALEXANDER JANNEUS

Antiochia
Seleucia
Hippus · Gamala
Philoteria · Dium
Dora · Gadara · Abila
Strato's Tower · Scythopolis
Pella
Samaria · Gerasa
Apollonia · Ammathus
Alexandrium
Adida
Gazara
Jerusalem
Hyrcania
Anthedon · Beth-zur · Macherus
Gaza
Raphia · Masada

■ Greek city under Janneus
Janneus' conquests

THE END OF JEWISH INDEPENDENCE

Damascus
SYRIA
Pompey's attack
Dium
JUDEA
Scythopolis · Pella
Coreae
Jericho
Jerusalem

the invitation. He marched into Judea by way of Coreae and Jericho, heading for Jerusalem.

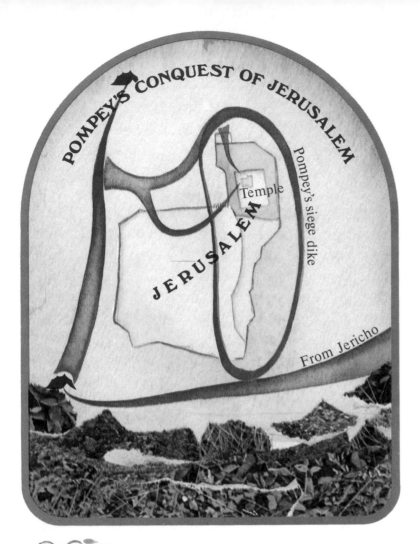

POMPEY'S CONQUEST OF JERUSALEM

JERUSALEM

Temple

Pompey's siege dike

From Jericho

THE RULE OF ROME

(Josephus, Antiquities 14–17
Jewish War 1–2)
63 BC – AD 6

At first it was Aristobulus who won Pompey's favour, but before long he found the Roman intervention going farther than he had bargained for, and tried to offer resistance. He barricaded himself in Jerusalem against the Romans, but when a Roman army arrived to lay siege to the city he thought better of it and gave himself up to them. The followers of Hyrcanus now won control of Jerusalem and opened its gates to the Romans. But the followers of Aristobulus retired to the temple area, which was separately fortified, and there they held out against a Roman siege for three months. At last the Romans broke into the sacred courts and crushed all remaining resistance. Pompey himself gratified his curiosity by entering the sanctuary itself, and even the holy of holies. Judea was now part of the Roman Empire (63 BC). It lost the Greek cities in the coastal plain.

Antipater, the supporter of Hyrcanus, saw it would be wise to work with the Romans, and this he did consistently until his death in 43 BC. Hyrcanus remained as high priest; he was also recognized as leader of the nation, but not as king.

Among the many services Antipater did for the Roman cause was organizing relief supplies for Julius Caesar when Caesar and Cleopatra were besieged in the palace quarter of Alexandria in the winter of 48–47 BC. Caesar showed his gratitude in many ways; his assassination in 44 BC was a blow to the Jews.

In 40 BC the Parthians from across the Euphrates invaded Syria and threw the Romans out. In Judea they installed as king and high priest a prince of the Hasmonean family named Antigonus. Antipater's son Herod knew that his life was in danger; he sent his family for safety to the rock-fortress of Masada, west of the Dead Sea, while he himself escaped to Rome. There the Roman senate proclaimed him king of the Jews; it was up to him to secure kingly power.

The Romans quickly recovered Syria from the Parthians; it was a slower business for Herod to recover Judea from Antigonus, who enjoyed wide popular support. After three years of warfare, which ended with a bitterly fought siege of Jerusalem, Herod gained control of the country and ruled it as king until his death in 4 BC.

In order to ensure the peace and prosperity of his kingdom, Herod made it his settled policy to support Rome. He was not, however, a popular ruler and his domestic life was most unhappy. He began to suspect everyone of trying to kill him. This led to the execution of his queen, Mariamne (a Hasmonean princess), in 29 BC, and of two of his sons by her in 7 BC. The last act of his life was to order the execution of his eldest son Antipater (his son by his first wife); Antipater's death took place only five days before his own.

The Roman rulers' confidence in Herod was shown by the repeated additions which they made to the territory over which he reigned. It came to include nearly all Palestine, with a district called Perea, east of the lower Jordan and Dead Sea, and a large region east and north-east of the Lake of Galilee. In many parts of his kingdom he built new cities or refounded old ones. Among the latter was the city of Samaria, which he renamed Sebaste in honour of the Emperor Augustus (Sebaste is the Greek equivalent of the Latin Augusta). On the Mediterranean coast he built the fine new harbour and seaport of Caesarea. He

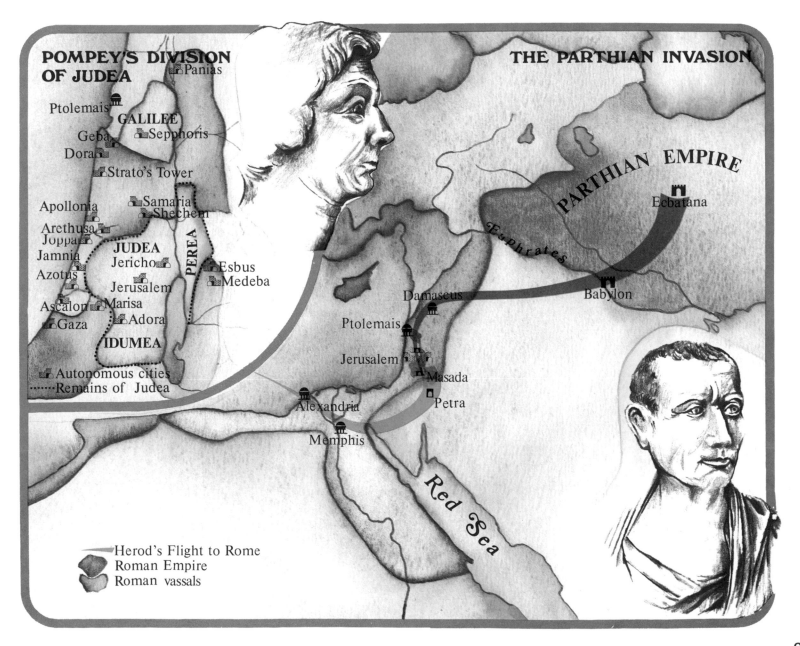

POMPEY'S DIVISION OF JUDEA

THE PARTHIAN INVASION

Panias

Ptolemais
GALILEE
Geba   Sepphoris
Dora
Strato's Tower

Apollonia   Samaria
            Shechem
Arethusa
Joppa
Jamnia   JUDEA   PEREA
          Jericho
Azotus   Jerusalem   Esbus
                       Medeba
Ascalon   Marisa
Gaza   Adora

IDUMEA

Autonomous cities
Remains of Judea

Alexandria

Memphis

PARTHIAN EMPIRE

Ecbatana

Euphrates

Babylon

Damascus

Ptolemais

Jerusalem

Masada

Petra

Red Sea

Herod's Flight to Rome
Roman Empire
Roman vassals

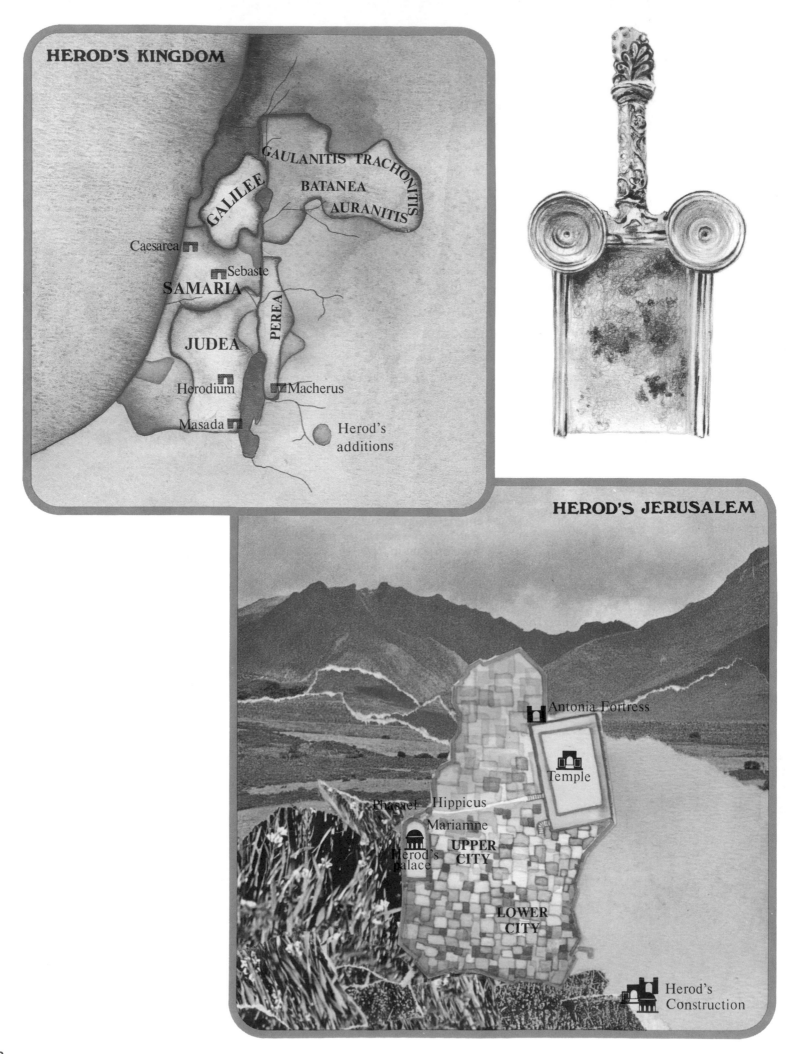

HEROD'S KINGDOM

GAULANITIS TRACHONITIS

GALILEE

BATANEA

AURANITIS

Caesarea

Sebaste

SAMARIA

PEREA

JUDEA

Herodium

Macherus

Masada

Herod's additions

HEROD'S JERUSALEM

Antonia Fortress

Temple

Phasael   Hippicus

Mariamne

Herod's palace

UPPER CITY

LOWER CITY

Herod's Construction

66

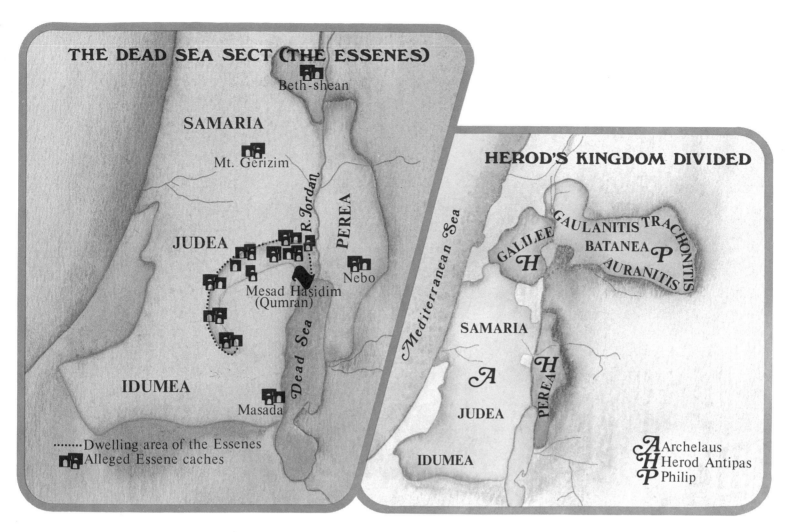

Beth-shean

SAMARIA

Mt. Gerizim

R. Jordan

PEREA

JUDEA

Nebo

Mesad Hasidim
(Qumran)

Dead Sea

IDUMEA

Masada

········ Dwelling area of the Essenes
Alleged Essene caches

HEROD'S KINGDOM DIVIDED

Mediterranean Sea

GALILEE
H

GAULANITIS TRACHONITIS
BATANEA *P*
AURANITIS

SAMARIA

A

PEREA

H

JUDEA

IDUMEA

A Archelaus
H Herod Antipas
P Philip

safeguarded the eastern part of his kingdom by building fortresses at Herodium, Masada and (in Perea) Macherus. His three-tiered palace on the rock of Masada is a wonder to behold even in its present ruined state. He adorned Jerusalem with fine new buildings – the royal palace on the western wall (where the citadel stands today), the fortress of Antonia north-west of the temple area, and (above all) the restoration and expansion of the temple. On this last work he spent a vast amount of money. A new temple was actually built, but since no interruption was caused in the daily services while the work was going on it continued to be known, religiously, as the second temple.

At Herod's death he left his kingdom to three of his sons, who were to divide it among themselves. His will was confirmed by the Emperor Augustus. Archelaus received Judea and Samaria. Antipas received Galilee and Perea, Philip received the region east and north-east of the Lake of Galilee. None of them received the title king: Archelaus was called ethnarch, while Antipas and Philip had to be content with the minor title of tetrarch. Antipas (called "Herod the tetrarch" in the New Testament) ruled his tetrarchy until AD 39 and Philip ruled his until his death in AD 34. But Archelaus, who had all his father's failings with none of his political ability, ruled so oppressively that there was danger of a rebellion among his subjects. Augustus therefore deposed him in AD 6. Judea (with Samaria) became a Roman province and was ruled by a governor appointed by the emperor.

Judea now had to pay tribute direct to the emperor's treasury. To fix the amount of taxation which might be expected from the new province, a census was held, under the direction of Quirinius, Roman governor of Syria. This caused the revolt led by Judas the Galilean, who inspired the later party of the Zealots. The payment of "tribute to Caesar" was to be a burning issue in Judea for the next sixty years.

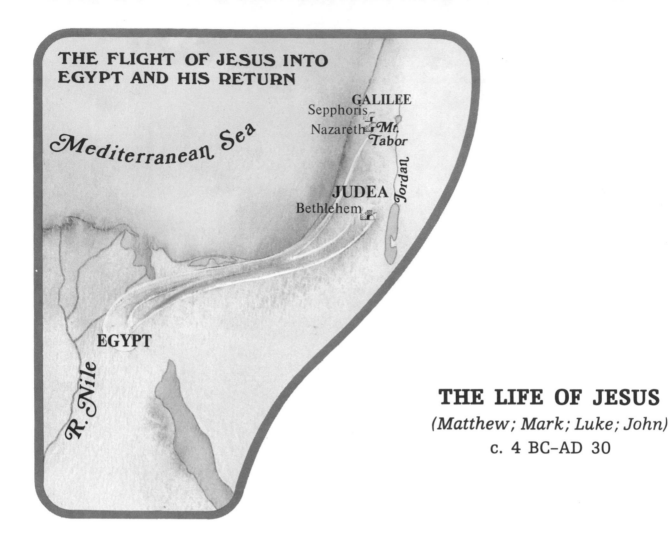

THE FLIGHT OF JESUS INTO EGYPT AND HIS RETURN

Mediterranean Sea

GALILEE
Sepphoris
Nazareth — Mt. Tabor

Jordan

JUDEA
Bethlehem

EGYPT

R. Nile

THE LIFE OF JESUS
(Matthew; Mark; Luke; John)
c. 4 BC–AD 30

Jesus was born towards the end of Herod's reign as king of the Jews. Matthew and Luke, the two gospel-writers who give an account of his birth, agree that he was born in Bethlehem. Matthew tells how his parents took him to Egypt to escape the danger threatened by Herod, who was disturbed by rumours that a new king of the Jews had been born. When, after Herod's death, they returned from Egypt, they did not settle in Bethlehem, which lay in the territory now controlled by Herod's son Archelaus. Instead, they moved north to Galilee and settled in Nazareth. There Jesus grew up from childhood to manhood. Indeed, it was in Galilee that Jesus spent most of his life.

When he was a boy of nine or ten years old, everybody around must have been talking of the revolt which Judas the Galilean had raised against the Romans in Judea. The Galileans were not directly affected by the revolt, nor by the census which sparked it off, for they paid their taxes to the tetrarch Herod Antipas, not to Caesar. But the news must have caused much excitement in Nazareth and other places in Galilee.

Nazareth lay rather off the beaten track, but the road from the Lake of Galilee to Ptolemais (Acco) ran a few miles to the north, while the Way of the Sea, connecting Egypt with Damascus and places farther north, passed by not far to the south. From the high ground above Nazareth many of the famous sites in the earlier history of Israel were to be seen.

In the earlier part of his rule, Herod Antipas had his court at Sepphoris, four miles north-north-west of Nazareth. Then, about AD 22, he built a new capital city for himself on the west shore of the Lake of Galilee, and called it Tiberias, in honour of the Emperor Tiberius, who had succeeded Augustus in AD 14. From the name of this city the lake came in due course to be called the Lake of Tiberias.

Jesus is not said to have visited either Sepphoris or Tiberias. But Sepphoris was so near Nazareth that rumours of goings-on at the tetrarch's court may have formed a background in the minds of Jesus' hearers when they listened to those parables of his in which kings and royal courts appeared.

It was usual for Jews from Galilee to journey to Jerusalem for one or another of a three great festivals of the year – Passover, Pentecost and Tabernacles. Luke tells how Jesus at the age of twelve was taken to Jerusalem at Passover, and how, when he went missing, he was found in discussion with some of the "scribes" or experts in the Jewish law who set up "schools" in the outer court of the temple at festival times, when Jerusalem was crowded with pilgrims.

Before Jesus began his public ministry, John the Baptist appeared. John, the son of a Judean priest, grew up to manhood in the wilderness of Judea where, about AD 27, he called the nation to repent. His preaching was powerful; he drew crowds from all parts of the country. Repentance was urgent, he said, because of the near approach of a person to whom he referred as the Coming One. The Coming One was going to carry out the divine judgment which would mark the end of the present age of wickedness and begin the coming age of righteousness. John's hearers were invited to show they had truly repented by being baptized by him in the Jordan. This was the setting in which Jesus' public activity began when he, for purposes of his own, asked John to baptize him and was assured, by a voice from heaven, that he was the Coming One whose way John was preparing. This assurance was confirmed by Jesus' experiences during the following forty days of fasting and testing. The traditional "Mount of Temptation" where he had those experiences is shown north-west of modern Jericho (due west of Tell es-Sultan).

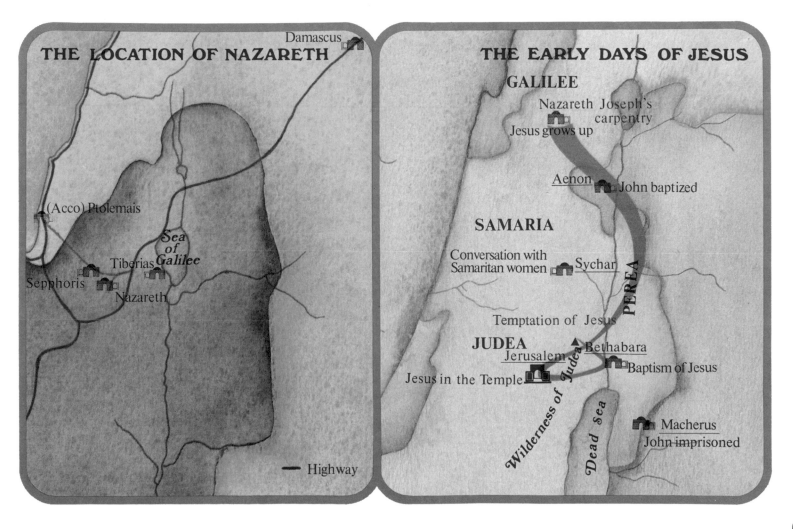

THE LOCATION OF NAZARETH

Damascus

(Acco) Ptolemais

Sea of Galilee

Tiberias

Sepphoris

Nazareth

— Highway

THE EARLY DAYS OF JESUS

GALILEE

Nazareth Joseph's carpentry
Jesus grows up

Aenon John baptized

SAMARIA

Conversation with Samaritan women   Sychar

PEREA

Temptation of Jesus

JUDEA   Bethabara
Jerusalem
Jesus in the Temple   Baptism of Jesus

Wilderness of Judea

Dead Sea

Macherus
John imprisoned

John went further, going into Samaria, and preaching at the well-watered site of Aenon near Salim (probably at the meeting place of the modern Wadi Baida and Wadi Far'a). But not long afterwards he was arrested in Antipas's Transjordanian territory of Perea and imprisoned in the fortress of Machaerus. There, after a few months, he was executed.

Jesus returned to Galilee, breaking his journey at a place in Samaria called Sychar. There he found some eager hearers among people who had recently been influenced by John the Baptist's preaching. When he arrived in Galilee, he made his headquarters at Capernaum and began to proclaim the good news that the kingdom of God was at hand. The kingdom of God was not a political organization; it meant the acceptance of the rule of God in the hearts of men and women, according to the principles laid down by Jesus in the Sermon on the Mount and on other occasions.

Capernaum was one of several flourishing fishing towns on the lake-shore. Others were Bethsaida, just east of the point where the Jordan flows into the lake, and Magdala, famed for its export of salt fish (for which reason it was also known as Taricheae). Other places

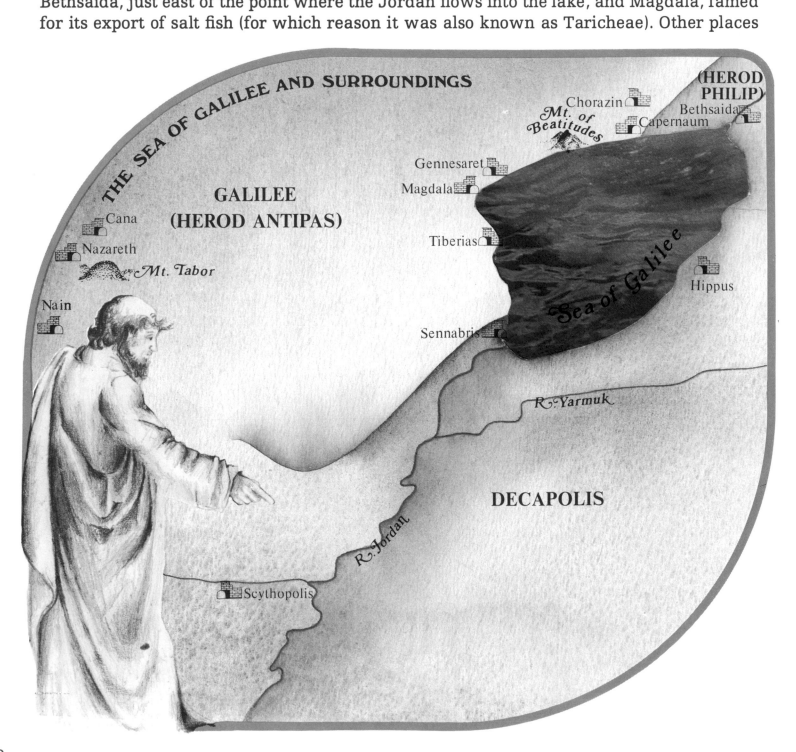

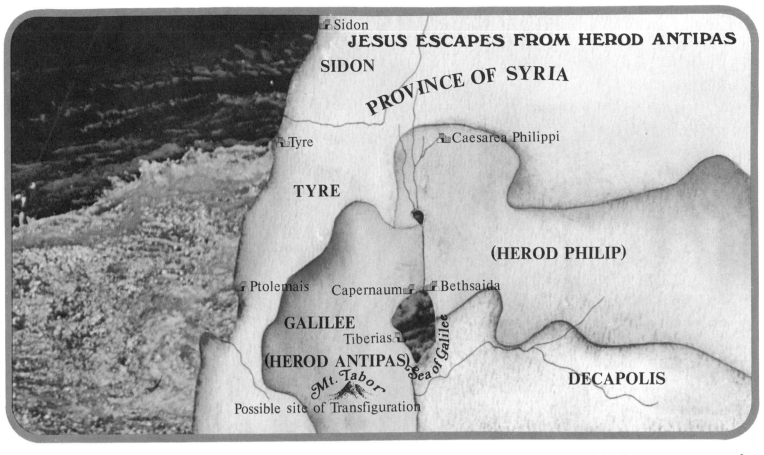

Sidon

SIDON

PROVINCE OF SYRIA

Tyre

Caesarea Philippi

TYRE

(HEROD PHILIP)

Ptolemais

Capernaum

Bethsaida

GALILEE

Tiberias

(HEROD ANTIPAS)

Mt. Tabor

Sea of Galilee

DECAPOLIS

Possible site of Transfiguration

mentioned in the narrative of his work in Galilee (in addition to his home town of Nazareth, where he met with a very cool reception) are Chorazin, a little way inland from Capernaum, Cana, where the water became wine (probably Khirbet Qana, about 9 miles north of Nazareth), and Nain, to the south of Mount Tabor. On the east side of the lake, at the place now called Kursi, the man possessed by a legion of demons was cured and the herd of pigs, feeding nearby, stampeded down the cliff into the lake.

The Sermon on the Mount was delivered, according to tradition, from the Mount of the Beatitudes, north-west of the lake. The land here forms a natural theatre, from which Jesus's words could have been heard a long way. Not only in this sermon but also in his parables Jesus explained in practical terms what the kingdom of God meant. The miracles, too – the works of mercy and power which also formed part of his ministry – were further visible signs of the kingdom of God. The way of life to be followed by those who wished to enter the kingdom of God was the way of life to be seen in Jesus himself.

Above all, the kingdom of God took its character from the God whose kingdom it was. Jesus taught his followers to think and speak of God as their Father, the liberal giver of all good things, who shows kindness and compassion even to those who do not deserve or appreciate his gifts. He taught them not only to place utter trust in God but to imitate him by showing kindness to others, even to the point of repaying evil with good. Where in consequence human beings behaved in such a way, the kingdom of God was present already, as it was present in his own person and work.

From among his followers, Jesus selected twelve for special responsibility. After instructing them, he sent them out two by two to preach the same good news throughout Galilee. Some weeks later they returned full of enthusiasm at what they reckoned to be a very successful mission. But in their enthusiasm they had roused the suspicion of Herod Antipas, who began to feel that in Jesus he had another John the Baptist on his hands.

Jesus took his disciples quickly across the lake, into the tetrarchy of Philip. Even there they were pursued by crowds from Galilee who, after Jesus had fed them with bread and

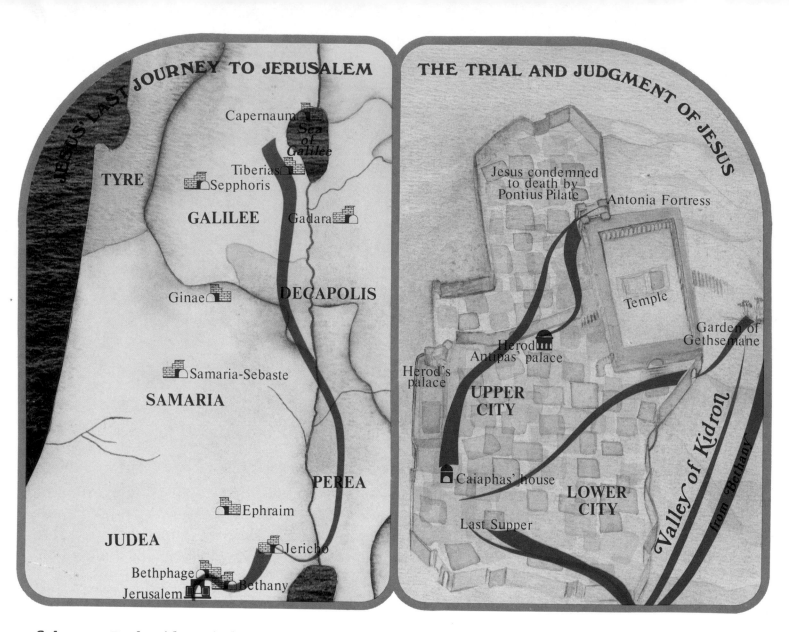

Capernaum
Sea of Galilee
TYRE
Tiberias
Sepphoris
GALILEE
Gadara
DECAPOLIS
Ginae
Samaria-Sebaste
SAMARIA
PEREA
Ephraim
JUDEA
Jericho
Bethphage
Jerusalem
Bethany

Jesus condemned to death by Pontius Pilate
Antonia Fortress
Temple
Garden of Gethsemane
Herod Antipas' palace
Herod's palace
UPPER CITY
Valley of Kidron
from Bethany
Caiaphas' house
LOWER CITY
Last Supper

fish near Bethsaida, tried to compel him to become their king. The kingdom of God, as they saw it, was an independent Jewish state, to be set up after a victorious war against the Romans and the Herods. Jesus taught people not to use violence nor return evil for evil. He would not attack the ruling powers with their own weapons. When he taught humility, meekness and self-denial this was indeed more revolutionary than anything the most extreme nationalists could think of. His example of serving others rather than receiving service himself, to the point of giving his life as "a ransom for many", a new way of resisting oppression.

The disciples themselves had been influenced by those who supported violence. Jesus therefore took them away into non-Jewish territory farther north, in the neighbourhood of Tyre and Sidon. There he gave them the intensive teaching that he thought they needed.

Towards the end of this period they came to Caesarea Philippi. This place was formerly called Panion, but Philip the tetrarch made it his capital and changed its name to Caesarea in honour of the Roman Emperor. (It was called Caesarea Philippi – that is, Philip's Caesarea – to distinguish it from the port of Caesarea on the Mediterranean). Here Peter, the spokesman of the twelve, spontaneously declared Jesus to be the Messiah. People were so used to thinking of the Messiah as a political and military leader that Jesus at once began to tell them how different his immediate future would be. He was shortly to go to Jerusalem with them, but instead of seeking armed victory and power there he would be arrested and put to death – and in this way he would complete his task.

On the last journey to Jerusalem, Jesus and his disciples seem to have gone through Transjordan and crossed the Jordan opposite Jericho. From Jericho they went up the steep, twisting road to Jerusalem. On this occasion, Jesus entered Jerusalem in a manner recalling an ancient prophecy where Zion's king comes to his city mounted on an ass and bringing a message of peace. He was received enthusiastically enough, although the enthusiasm came more from Galilean pilgrims who had reached the city ahead of him than to the Jerusalemites themselves.

The temple-rulers in Jerusalem knew that their privileges depended on continued cooperation with the Roman power, but the common people would have welcomed a deliverer to defeat Rome. Within the next few days it became plain that Jesus had no intention of being that kind of deliverer. He would not even denounce the payment of taxes to the Roman Emperor (which was a token of submission to his rule). He did indeed expel traders from the outer court of the temple, but this was the action of a prophet, not of a rebel leader. Popular enthusiasm for him quickly cooled, but the chief priests, for fear that he might provoke a rising, had already arranged to have him arrested. One of his disciples, Judas Iscariot, had promised to show them where to lay hands on him without danger of a riot.

Accordingly, on the Thursday evening of Passover Week Jesus was arrested, tried early next morning before the Roman governor Pontius Pilate, and condemned to death for encouraging rebellion and claiming to be "king of the Jews". The death-sentence was carried out by crucifixion, and it looked as if the movement led by Jesus had gone the same way as other ill-fated movements which were started in Judea under the Romans.

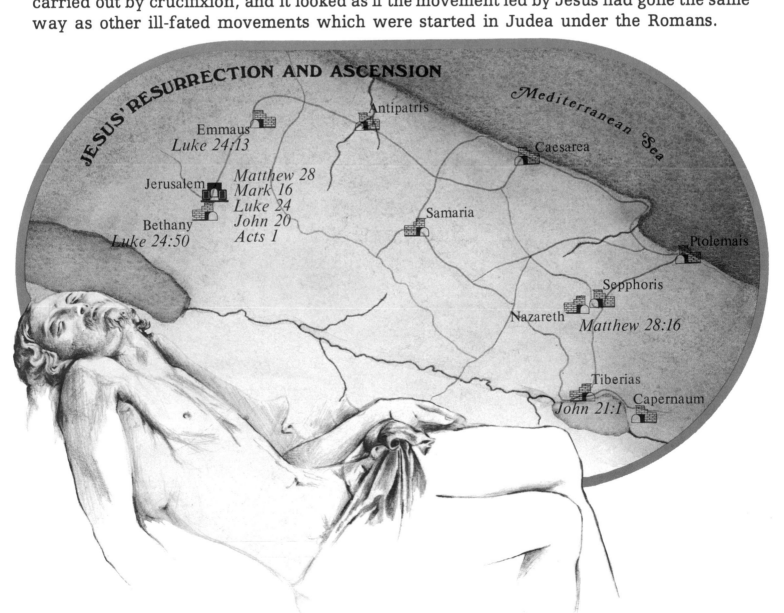

JESUS' RESURRECTION AND ASCENSION

Mediterranean Sea

Antipatris

Emmaus
Luke 24:13

Caesarea

Jerusalem

Matthew 28
Mark 16
Luke 24
John 20
Acts 1

Bethany
Luke 24:50

Samaria

Ptolemais

Sepphoris

Nazareth   Matthew 28:16

Tiberias
Capernaum
John 21:1

THE BEGINNINGS OF CHRISTIANITY

(Acts; The New Testament Letters)

AD 30–70

The movement started by Jesus did not come to an end with his death. On the contrary, within ten years it had spread far beyond the boundaries of the Holy Land; within twenty years it was established in Rome and Alexandria.

This expansion would never have begun if Jesus had not risen from death and appeared alive again to many of his disciples. Because of this they shared what is called the resurrection faith, but this faith depended on the fact that Jesus really had risen.

A few weeks after Jesus's crucifixion, some of his followers in Jerusalem spoke publicly to a crowd of pilgrims who had come from all parts of the Roman Empire for the feast of Pentecost. They announced that Jesus had not only risen from death but had been exalted by God to be ruler over the whole universe and that he had given them the right to offer forgiveness of sins and the gift of the indwelling Spirit of God to all who confessed him as Lord. An increasing number of people did so, and formed a community of believers in Jesus – mainly in Jerusalem but also in some other centres in Judea. The leaders of this new movement won popular good will by performing acts of healing such as had marked Jesus's ministry and also by attending the temple services regularly and by keeping the Jewish religious rules. In fact, they observed them more closely than their Master had done.

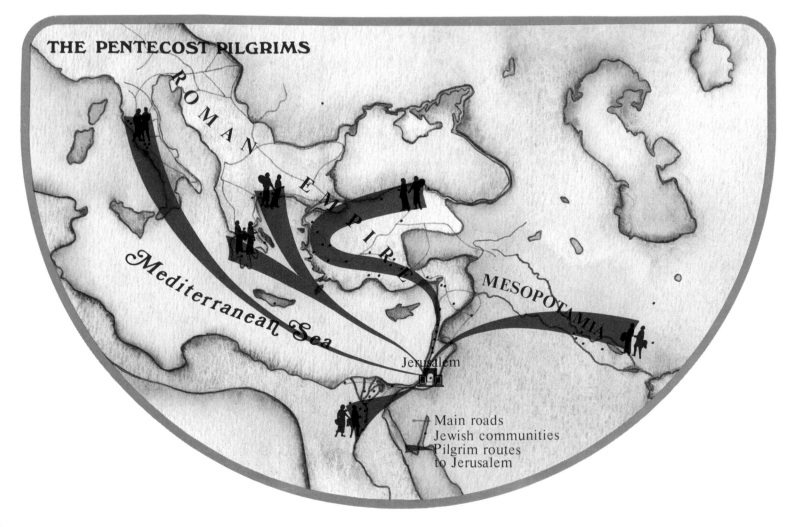

THE PENTECOST PILGRIMS

ROMAN EMPIRE

Mediterranean Sea

MESOPOTAMIA

Jerusalem

Main roads
Jewish communities
Pilgrim routes
to Jerusalem

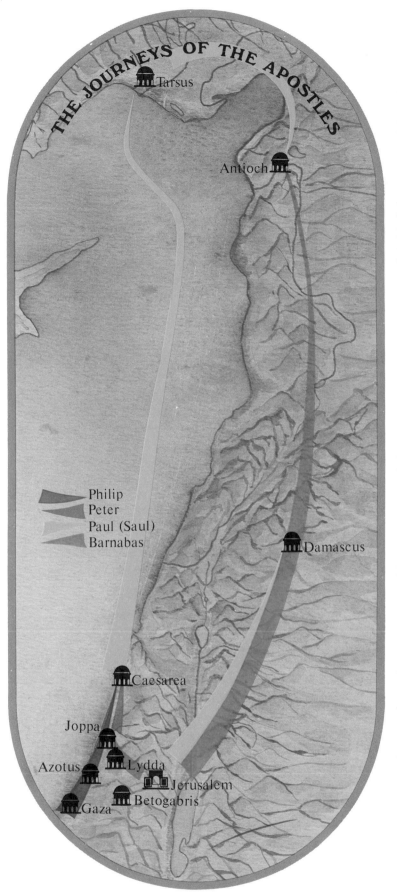

THE JOURNEYS OF THE APOSTLES

Tarsus

Antioch

Philip
Peter
Paul (Saul)
Barnabas

Damascus

Caesarea

Joppa

Azotus   Lydda

Gaza   Betogabris

Jerusalem

Among the Jews of Judea were some called Hellenists, who had links with Jewish communities in the eastern Mediterranean provinces outside the Holy Land, who normally spoke Greek and attended synagogues where the service was conducted in Greek. A number of Hellenists joined the new movement. They kept less to Jewish traditions: some, indeed, thought that the temple, with its priesthood and sacrifices, had outlived whatever usefulness it formerly had. They could claim that several of the great prophets of Israel and, in some degree, Jesus himself had shared this view. One Hellenistic leader, Stephen, stated these ideas publicly and found himself in court on a charge of blasphemy. Blasphemy was a capital offence, and Stephen was found guilty and executed by stoning. All who had worked with him – mainly, but not only, Hellenists like himself – now came under attack from the authorities, with popular approval.

This led to their dispersal from Judea into neighbouring regions. But the dispersed Hellenists spread the message of Jesus – the gospel – wherever they went, at first only to their fellow-Jews but soon to non-Jews, Gentiles, as well. This was particularly so in the great city of Antioch in North Syria, where a largely Gentile church (a community of believers in Jesus) came into being. It was the people of Antioch who called the followers of Jesus "Christians".

In Judea itself a small group of Gentile Christians was formed in the seaport of Caesarea (the headquarters of the Roman governor of the province), where another leader of the Christian Hellenists, Philip, who had taken the gospel to the people of Samaria, made his home for many years. The first member of this group actually belonged to the Roman army: he was a centurion named Cornelius, a convert not of Philip but of Peter.

The most noteworthy convert in those early days was a young Jew called Paul, a native of Tarsus in Cilicia, educated at Jerusalem in the academy of Gamaliel the elder, the greatest rabbi of his day. Paul was at first fiercely opposed to the Christians. When he was

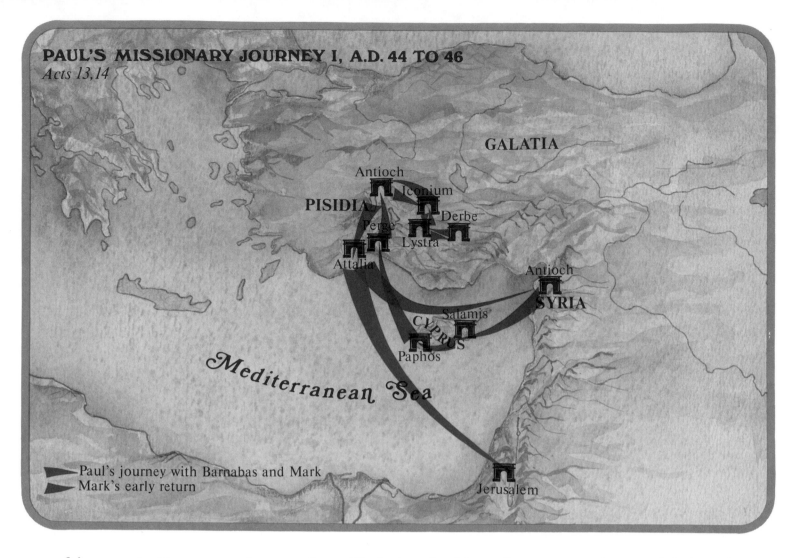

GALATIA

Antioch
Iconium
PISIDIA
Derbe
Perge
Lystra

Attalia

Antioch
SYRIA

Salamis
CYPRUS
Paphos

Mediterranean Sea

Paul's journey with Barnabas and Mark
Mark's early return

Jerusalem

on his way to Damascus to round up Christian fugitives from Jerusalem and bring them back for trial, he was confronted by the risen Christ and called to be his servant and messenger in the Gentile world.

Paul was neither the first nor the only Christian missionary to the Gentile world, but he gave himself so wholeheartedly to this work that something new was added to the Christian movement. In the first few years of his Christian career he was active mainly in Syria and Cilicia. Barnabas, whom the leaders of the Jerusalem church sent to Antioch to supervise the preaching of the gospel to the Gentiles there, enlisted Paul as his helper in this work. From Antioch about AD 46 Barnabas and Paul began to take the gospel to Cyprus and central Asia Minor. A large part of central Asia Minor was occupied by the province of Galatia, in which several churches were planted at this time, consisting in the main of believing Gentiles.

Christianity began within the Jewish religion. But now the number of Gentiles in it was growing fast, and the founder-members faced a problem. Should Christianity continue as part of the Jewish religion? If so, Gentile converts must observe Jewish customs. On the other hand, if Gentile converts were to be free from such requirements, if the confession of Jesus as Lord was the only condition for membership in the Christian community, there would be a tendency for Jewish Christians also not to keep the Jewish law so strictly, and the breach between church and synagogue would be widened.

A special meeting was held at Jerusalem to deal with the question. While the more conservative members of the Jerusalem church wanted Gentile Christians to keep all the Jewish laws, the meeting decided it would be enough if they kept the most important ones, about marriage and food.

Paul himself took a more liberal line: he would impose no food-restrictions but encouraged Jewish and Gentile Christians to show each other consideration and courtesy. He thought it important to keep good relations with the Jerusalem church, but these inevitably continued to be strained.

However, Paul went on taking the Gospel to the Gentiles: between AD 47 and 57 he established Christian churches in the chief cities of four provinces: Galatia, Asia, Macedonia and Achaia. Special mention is made in Acts of the churches of Philippi, Thessalonica, Corinth (where Paul spent 18 months) and Ephesus (where he spent nearly three years).

In order to strengthen the sense of unity between those churches and the mother church in Jerusalem, Paul organized a collection of money throughout his Gentile mission-field for the relief of the poverty of the Jerusalem Christians. Early in AD 57 he himself, with representatives of the contributing churches, travelled to Jerusalem to hand over the money to the leaders of the Jerusalem church, chief among whom was James the Just, the brother of Jesus.

The gift was no doubt welcome, but in the eyes of many Jerusalemites Paul was a traitor to Judaism. While he was in Jerusalem he was set upon by an enraged mob because of a rumour that he had broken the sacred laws of the temple. He was rescued and taken prisoner by the Roman garrison in the Antonia fortress. From Jerusalem he was sent to Caesarea, the home of Felix, the Roman governor of Judea. There, two years later, he put an end to official delays over his case by appealing to be tried at Rome before the emperor.

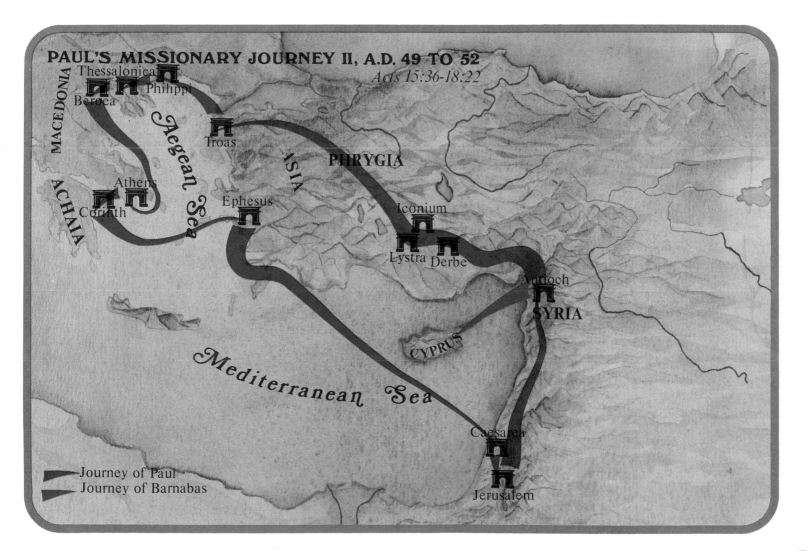

PAUL'S MISSIONARY JOURNEY II, A.D. 49 TO 52
Acts 15:36-18:22

Journey of Paul
Journey of Barnabas

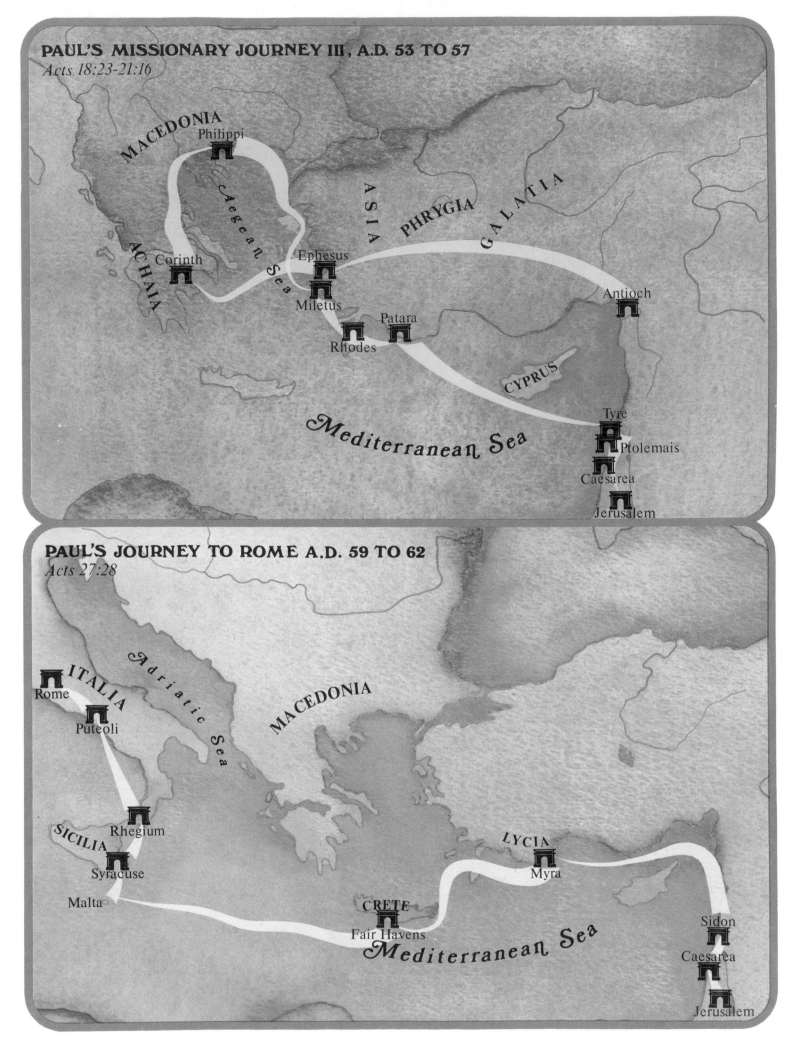

PAUL'S MISSIONARY JOURNEY III, A.D. 53 TO 57
Acts 18:23-21:16

MACEDONIA
Philippi

Aegean Sea

ASIA
PHRYGIA
GALATIA

ACHAIA
Corinth

Ephesus
Miletus
Patara
Rhodes

Antioch

CYPRUS

Mediterranean Sea

Tyre
Ptolemais
Caesarea
Jerusalem

PAUL'S JOURNEY TO ROME A.D. 59 TO 62
Acts 27:28

Adriatic Sea

ITALIA
Rome
Puteoli

MACEDONIA

Aegean Sea

SICILIA
Rhegium
Syracuse
Malta

LYCIA
Myra

CRETE
Fair Havens

Mediterranean Sea

Sidon
Caesarea
Jerusalem

78

This was his right as a Roman citizen. Early in AD 60 he reached Rome after an eventful journey.

Although Jesus was executed by sentence of a Roman judge on a charge of encouraging rebellion, his followers, and particularly Paul, found many Roman authorities treated them quite fairly. During Paul's stay in Corinth (AD 50–52), Gallio, proconsul of Achaia, gave a ruling which in practice declared Christianity to be part of the Jewish religion; as such it shared the permission which Roman law granted for the practice of that religion.

Paul profited by Gallio's ruling for ten years, even in Rome itself, where he spent two years under house-arrest waiting for his case to come up for trial and preaching the gospel freely to all who cared to visit him. At last, however, the difference between Jews and Christians was plain for all to see, and Christianity was no longer protected by law. When the Emperor Nero looked around for scapegoats to bear the blame for the great fire which ruined much of Rome in the summer of AD 64, he found it easy to divert the popular

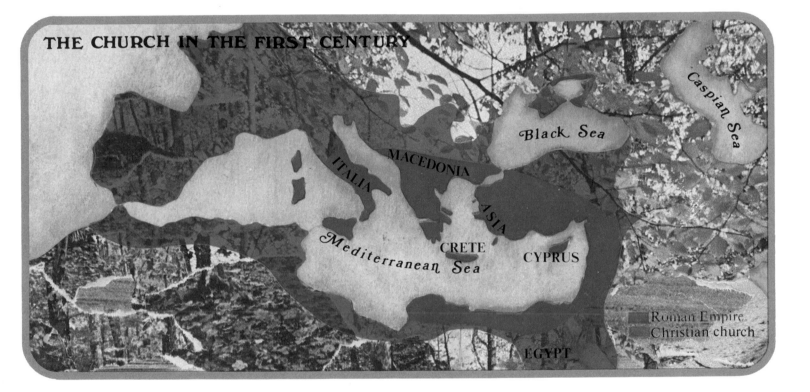

THE CHURCH IN THE FIRST CENTURY

indignation against the Christians of the city. In the resulting persecution, according to tradition, both Paul and Peter were put to death.

Another Christian leader, James the Just, met his death in the 60s. He was executed by stoning, along with some others, by the illegal action of the high priest Ananus when there was temporarily no Roman governor in Judea. James's death (AD 62) was a blow to the church of Jerusalem, from which it never recovered. A few years later the church left Jerusalem about the time of the Judean revolt against Rome (AD 66); most of its members settled beyond the Jordan, and no longer played an important part in the history of Christianity.

From now on there was no further question of maintaining a balance between the Jewish-Christian church in Jerusalem and the mainly Gentile church throughout the world. The church survived its first clash with the imperial power of Rome (under Nero) and continued to expand until, 250 years later, the imperial power (under Constantine) yielded to it.

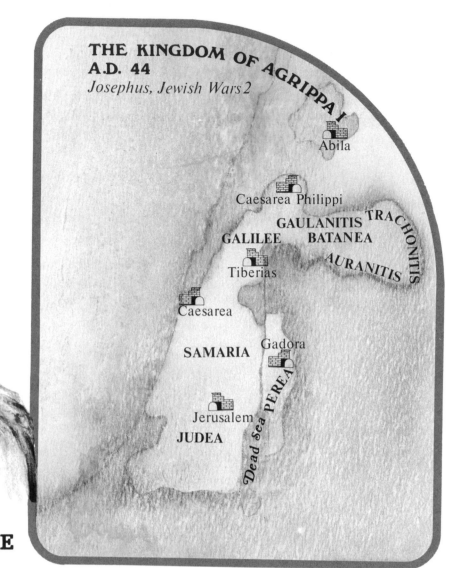

**THE KINGDOM OF AGRIPPA I
A.D. 44**
Josephus, Jewish Wars 2

Abila

Caesarea Philippi

GAULANITIS **TRACHONITIS**
GALILEE **BATANEA**
AURANITIS
Tiberias

Caesarea

SAMARIA Gadora

PEREA
Jerusalem *Dead sea*
JUDEA

THE REVOLTS OF
THE JEWS AGAINST ROME
(Josephus, Jewish War 2-7)
AD 66–74; 132–135

Life under Roman governors could not in any case have been easy for the Jews of Judea. It meant paying heavy taxes. They had to pay tribute to Caesar, and at the same time they had to go on paying "tithes" (ten per cent of their income) and other dues for the maintenance of the temple in Jerusalem. But the type of man who was regularly sent out as governor did not make them feel that Roman protection was something worth paying for. Some of them took no care to respect the religious feelings of the Jews; some were harsh and oppressive. This meant that the arguments of those who shared the earlier vision of Judas the Galilean found ready ears.

There was a welcome relief between AD 41 and 44. In the former year the Emperor Claudius came to power in Rome and, instead of sending a Roman governor to Judea, he appointed an old classmate of his, a grandson of Herod Agrippa. His subjects were happy under his rule, but he died after three years. His son, the younger Herod Agrippa, was only seventeen years old, and Claudius was advised that such a difficult province as Judea should not be entrusted to a ruler of such a tender age. So once more Roman governors were appointed.

About this time there was a revival of the activity of guerrilla nationalists – the kind of people who nowadays are called freedom fighters by their own side and terrorists by the other. They were put down ruthlessly by the Romans, but nothing was done to relieve the conditions which encouraged people to rebel. When, however, revolt at last broke out on a national scale, it was not those fighters (now called the Zealots) who took the lead but the captain of the temple, who belonged to the chief-priestly family. He ended the daily sacrifice on behalf of the emperor which had been offered in the temple for many years: this was in effect a declaration of war.

The Zealots now saw their opportunity; they stormed the Antonia fortress and massacred the Roman garrison which had its headquarters there. They had already seized the fortress of Masada, where they were to hold out for eight years.

The Roman governor of Syria, Cestius Gallus, marched south with the twelfth legion and auxiliary forces, but found that even so the situation could not be brought under control. He withdrew and suffered heavy losses when his troops were ambushed in the Pass of Beth-horon (November, AD 66). The Jews then set up their own government and divided the country into military regions. A veteran general, Vespasian, was sent to Judea with enough soldiers to re-conquer it district by district. By the end of spring in AD 68 he had re-established Roman control over most of the country. In June of that year Nero was forced to take his own life and a struggle about who should succeed him broke out in Rome. Vespasian took no further action until he saw the outcome of this struggle.

The outcome was his own return to Rome as emperor in the later part of AD 69. He left his son Titus in Judea to complete the suppression of the revolt. Titus besieged Jerusalem in April, AD 70. The defenders held out stubbornly against him, but the temple was set on fire at the end of August and a month later the whole city was in Titus's hands. In a few places resistance continued but these were overcome one by one. First Herodium and then Macherus were taken. The last to fall was Masada, where the Zealots garrison and their families committed mass suicide in April, AD 74, rather than fall into the hands of the Romans.

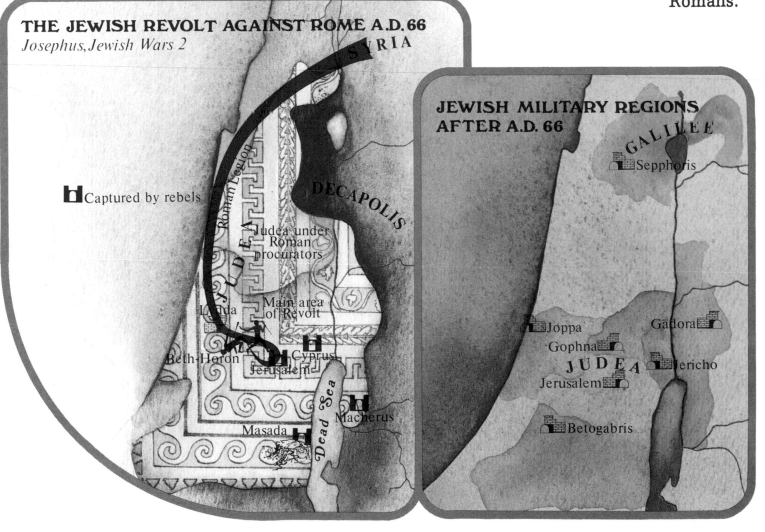

THE JEWISH REVOLT AGAINST ROME A.D. 66
Josephus, Jewish Wars 2

SYRIA

Captured by rebels

Roman Legion

DECAPOLIS

Judea under Roman procurators

JUDEA

Main area of Revolt

Lydda

Beth-Horon

Cyprus

Jerusalem

Dead Sea

Masada

Macherus

JEWISH MILITARY REGIONS AFTER A.D. 66

GALILEE

Sepphoris

Joppa

Gophna

Gadora

JUDEA

Jericho

Jerusalem

Betogabris

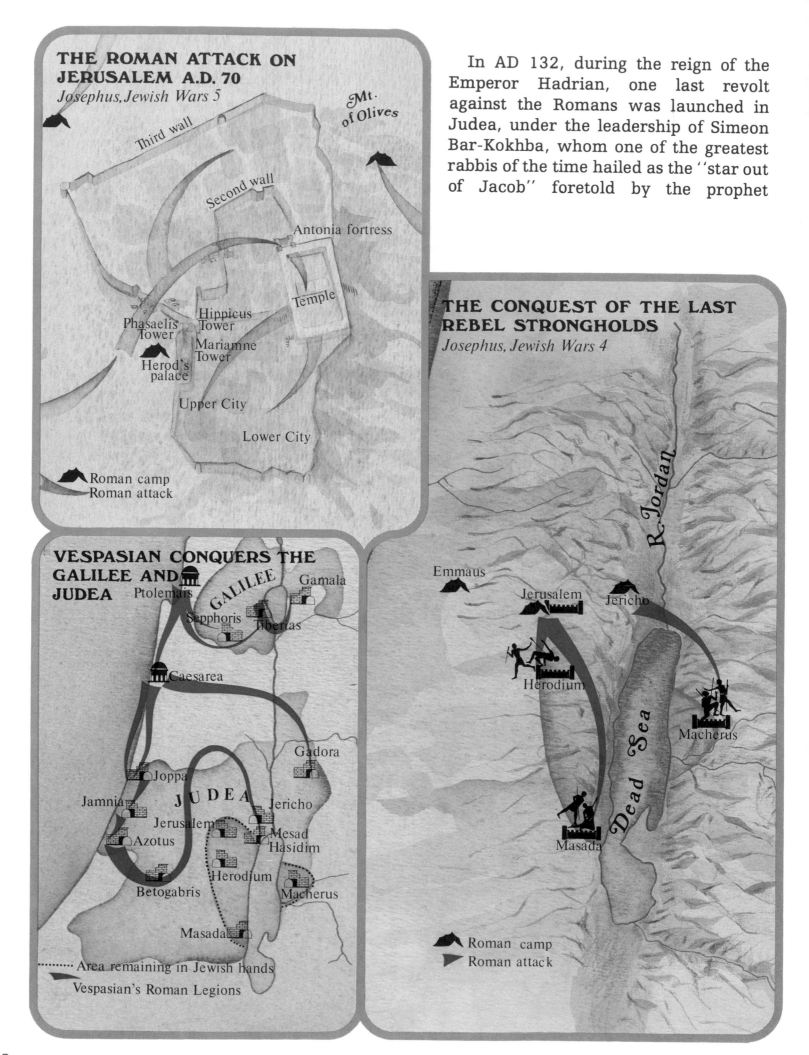

THE ROMAN ATTACK ON JERUSALEM A.D. 70
Josephus, Jewish Wars 5

Mt. of Olives

Third wall

Second wall

Antonia fortress

Temple

Hippicus Tower

Phasaelis Tower

Mariamne Tower

Herod's palace

Upper City

Lower City

▲ Roman camp
◄ Roman attack

In AD 132, during the reign of the Emperor Hadrian, one last revolt against the Romans was launched in Judea, under the leadership of Simeon Bar-Kokhba, whom one of the greatest rabbis of the time hailed as the ''star out of Jacob'' foretold by the prophet

THE CONQUEST OF THE LAST REBEL STRONGHOLDS
Josephus, Jewish Wars 4

R. Jordan

Emmaus

Jerusalem

Jericho

Herodium

Dead Sea

Macherus

Masada

▲ Roman camp
◄ Roman attack

VESPASIAN CONQUERS THE GALILEE AND JUDEA

GALILEE

Ptolemais

Gamala

Sepphoris

Tiberias

Caesarea

Gadora

Joppa

Jamnia

J U D E A

Jericho

Jerusalem

Azotus

Mesad Hasidim

Herodium

Betogabris

Macherus

Masada

········· Area remaining in Jewish hands
◄ Vespasian's Roman Legions

Balaam over 1,000 years before. For three years Bar-Kokhba was able to maintain an independent Jewish state in Judea. Fresh light was thrown on him and his campaigns in 1952, when letters from him were discovered in a cave in the Wadi Murabba'at, west of the Dead Sea, which served as one of his military outposts. But his bid for independence did not succeed: once again fresh Roman reinforcements arrived in Judea. Although the rebels took refuge in the fortress of Bethther, south-west of Jerusalem, the revolt was crushed and those who had been in any way involved in it were made to suffer. Not until the twentieth century (1948) was an independent Jewish state again established in the Holy Land.

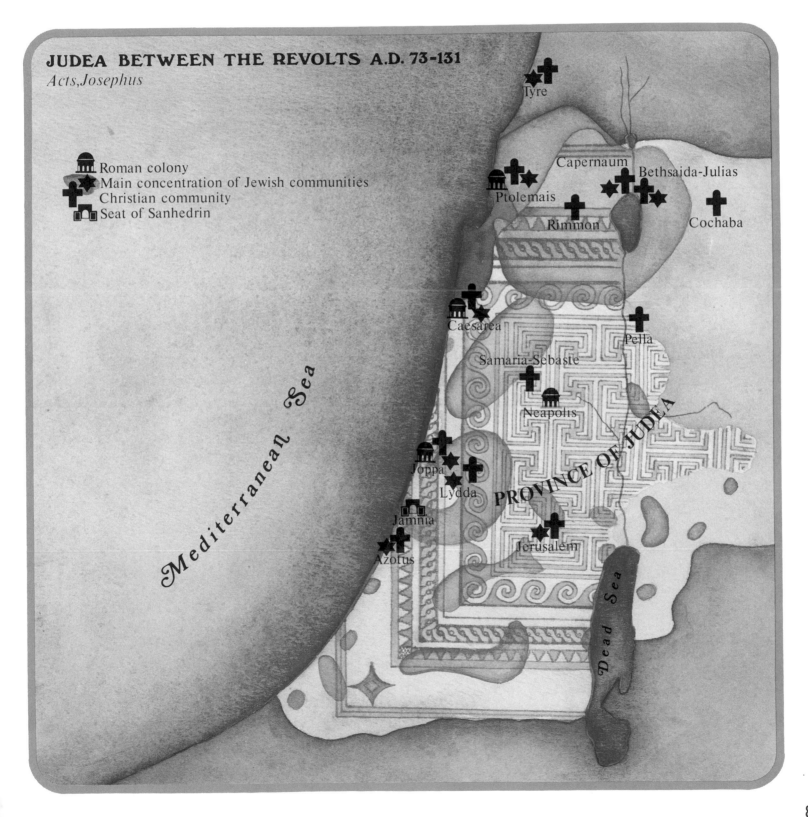

JUDEA BETWEEN THE REVOLTS A.D. 73-131
Acts, Josephus

Roman colony
Main concentration of Jewish communities
Christian community
Seat of Sanhedrin

Tyre

Capernaum
Bethsaida-Julias

Ptolemais
Rimmon
Cochaba

Mediterranean Sea

Caesarea
Pella

Samaria-Sebaste

Neapolis

PROVINCE OF JUDEA

Joppa
Lydda

Jamnia

Jerusalem

Azotus

Dead Sea

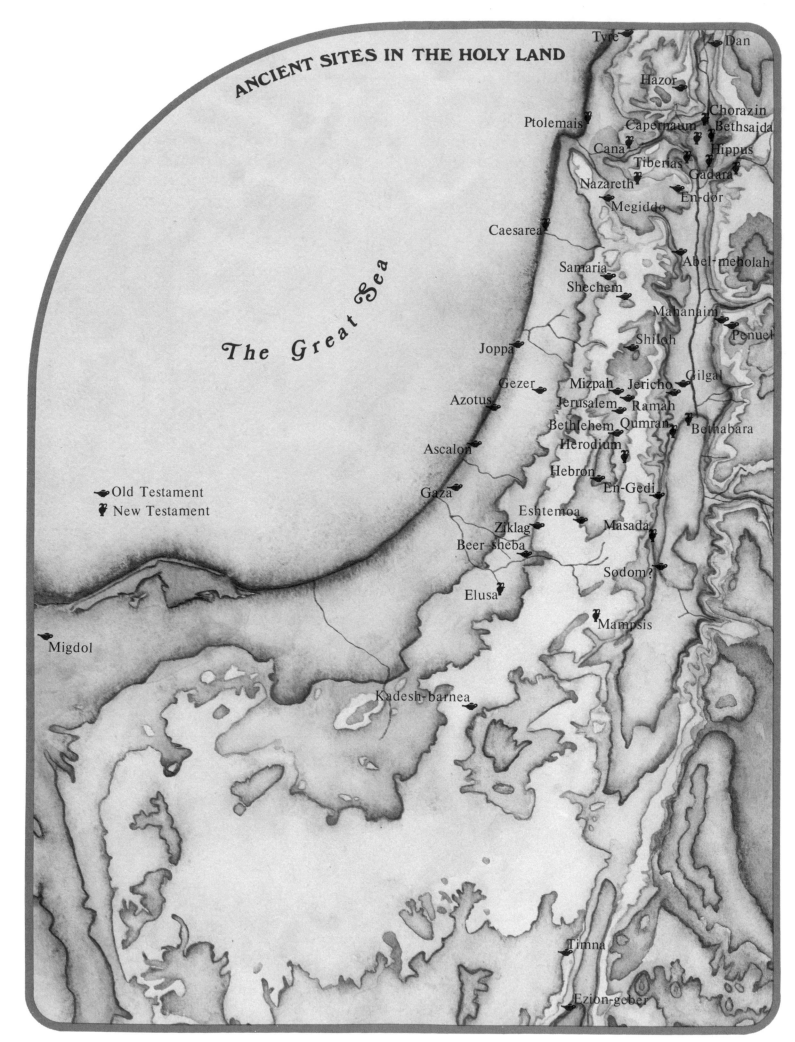

ANCIENT SITES IN THE HOLY LAND

Tyre
Dan
Hazor
Chorazin
Ptolemais
Capernaum
Bethsaida
Cana
Hippus
Tiberias
Gadara
Nazareth
En-dor
Megiddo
Caesarea
Abel-meholah
Samaria
Shechem
Mahanaim
Shiloh
Penuel
Joppa
Gezer
Mizpah
Jericho
Gilgal
Azotus
Jerusalem
Ramah
Bethlehem
Qumran
Bethabara
Herodium
Ascalon
Hebron
En-Gedi
Gaza
Eshtemoa
Masada
Ziklag
Beer-sheba
Sodom?
Elusa
Mampsis
Migdol
Kadesh-barnea
Timna
Ezion-geber

The Great Sea

Old Testament
New Testament

Index

A

Abdon 22
Abel-beth-maacah 37, 40
Abel-meholah 40, 84
Abel-shittim 18
Abila 63, 80
Acco 20, (Ptolemais 69)
Achaia 77, 78
Achshaph 19
Achzib 20
Acrabeta 60
Adida 63
Adora 65
Adullam 30, 42, 50, 53
Adriatic Sea 78
Aegean Sea 21, 77, 78
Aenon 69
Ahlab 20
Ahaz 48
Ai 12, 19
Aijalon 20, 32, 42
Akhetaton 13
Akkad 9
Alexandria 56, 65
Alexandrium 63
Amalekites 28, 29, 31
Ammathus 63
Ammon 20, 24, 32, 34, 35, 36, 37, 40, 42,
   47, 48
Anthedon 63
Antioch 56, 75, 76, 77, 78
Antiochia 59, 63
Antiochia (Hippus) 59
Antiochia Jerusalem 59
Antipatris 73
Aphek 20, 31, 44, 50, 53
Apollonia 59, 63, 65
Arabah 16, 34
Arabia 39, 45, 56
Arabian Desert 8, 10
Arad 38
Aram-Damascus 35, 37, 40, 42, 43, 44,
   45, 48
Aram-Zobah 34, 35
Arethusa 65

Argob 40
Aroer 40, 47
Arvad 45
Asa 43
Ascalon 65, 84
Ashan 38
Ashdod 21, 25, 26
Ashkelon 21, 25
Asher 20, 29, 32, 37
Asia 77, 78, 79
Asia Minor 21
Aswan 13
Ashtaroth 40, 47
Assyria 11, 45, 46, 49, 52
Assyrian Empire 51
Athens 77
Attalia 76
Auranitis 66, 67, 80
Avaris 13, 15
Ayalon, Valley of 19
Azekah 19, 29, 32, 42, 53
Azotus 59, 60, 65, 75, 82, 83, 84
Azotus Paralius 59

B

Baalath-beer 38
Baal-hazor 36
Baal-meon 60
Baal-perazim 32
Baal-zephon 15
Baasha 43
Babylon 9, 10, 49, 51, 52, 53, 54, 56, 65
Babylonian Empire 52, 54
Bahurim 36
Barak 22
Bashan 16, 40
Batanea 66, 67, 80
Beautitudes, Mt. of 70
Beer-lahai-roi 12
Beeroth 19
Beer-sheba 12, 35, 38, 53, 84
Benjamin 20, 24, 26, 27, 28, 29, 32, 37
Beroea 77
Bethabara 69, 84
Beth-anath 20

ILLUSTRATIONS